D1533759

HELLO HAROLD

HAROLD EVENSKY, CFP

Print ISBN: 978-1-54390-059-0

eBook ISBN: 978-1-62452-148-5

Copyright © Harold Evensky 2017

License Notes

All rights reserved. No part of this ebook may be reproduced in any form or by any means without prior written permission from the publisher except for brief quotations embodied in critical essay, article or review. These articles and/or review must state the correct title and contributing authors of this book by name.

INTRODUCTION

Welcome to *Hello Harold* (that's me, Harold Evensky). I've been a practicing financial planner for over three decades; financial planning is my avocation as well as my vocation. I've had the privilege of participating in the growth of my profession, serving on the national Board of the International Association for Financial Planning, as Chair of the Certified Financial Planning Board, the International Certified Financial Planning Board of Standards, as well as on advisory boards for Charles Schwab and TIAA-CREF.

In those three decades plus, I've seen a great many changes, not only in the markets but also in how investors—and their advisors—respond to them. Some of those responses make very little sense. Financial planning is a powerful tool that can help you develop and maintain the quality of life you want. Unfortunately, there's a ton of noise and nonsense foisted on investors that can undermine their financial success.

Maybe you're one of the many unlucky folks who've tried using a broker or financial advisor and wound up with one of the few less than ethical ones who had you invest in easy-answer funds that did more for the advisor's bottom line than yours. Maybe you decided to go it alone. Unfortunately, investing is not a simple task and without a grasp of the fundamentals many investors wind up making costly mistakes. Although there are innumerable books—many of them very good—designed to help you invest wisely, many are too long, too technical, too boring, too commercial, or too simplistic to hold the reader's attention.

So it's my turn. I decided my book would be just right—not too long, not too short, not too technical, not too simplistic, not commercial and, most important, fun to read. *Hello Harold* gives you the foundation you need to navigate the markets and plan your financial future. I take you along with me on phone calls and meetings, conferences and classrooms, and let you eavesdrop on my thoughts, conversations, and brainstorming sessions with clients, colleagues, and students. I introduce you to actionable concepts that will make you a far better investor, with a sound plan for your future. You may even have some fun along the way.

Unlike most books you're familiar with, don't feel obligated to move from page one through to the end. Each chapter stands on its own, so you can skip and jump to your heart's content, chasing subjects you find of interest in any order that appeals to you. No matter where you land, whether it's cash flow or market timing or taxes or any of a myriad of essential topics, you're likely to find something you hadn't considered before in quite that way. Each chapter is designed to give you insights that will improve your financial bottom line and your chances of achieving your financial goals.

Contents

PART 1:

ALL ABOUT THE MARKETS, INVESTMENTS, AND PORTFOLIO DESIGN

CHAPTER 1

'WHAT A GREAT COMPANY! I'LL BUY THE STOCK!'

———————◆———————

How to Decide If You Really Should

If you're managing your own portfolio, there are temptations that can lead you astray and cause you to veer away from the investment strategy you've settled on, and cost you a lot of money. For example: sooner or later you're bound to hear a story about a company that's headed for success—a great investment. The tip may come from a friend, a neighbor, an article you've read, or even a new acquaintance at a bar. And if you have some funds available, it's awfully tempting to think about investing in your new *find*.

That's the moment to step back—and beware. You might be falling into a classic investment trap. One of my clients—let's call him David Samuel—came close to learning this the hard way.

David Samuel (DS): Hello, Harold. It's David Samuel. I need your advice.

Harold Evensky (HE): Well, good morning, David. It's been a while. How was your trip to Key West with the kids?

DS: Absolutely terrific! Actually, that's the reason for the call. I did some wandering around while we were down there. The boys spent all their time on mopeds so I had to tool around on my own.

HE: Whoa! David, are you telling me you were on a moped?!

DS: What's the matter, don't you believe it? Ha! I was just like James Dean, I mean cool! Anyway, I met a fellow named Pin Stripe Tout Morgan at the Casa Marina bar. He's a real player and he let me in on a great opportunity. I'm sure it's a winner. I'm ready to buy it, but I want to know what you think.

HE: Is this *the* David Samuel asking me this? The one who sees an opportunity approximately twelve times a day? Well, so far, you haven't exactly overwhelmed me with new information. You tell *me* why you should buy it.

DS: Harold, this stock is just so exciting I was sure you'd agree with me. Tout says Super Tech is a great buy (and remember, this is confidential, *very* confidential). The company produces a revolutionary computer! Our office just bought ten of their new units and our neighbor just ordered four for his office.

HE: Anything else?

DS: Sure, I've been watching the tech stocks and their share price has been going straight up. Besides, the whole world depends on technology.

HE: How much are you going to buy?

DS: Oh, I figure I'll spend about $50,000 of my IRA funds on it.

HE: David, that's *all* of your IRA.

DS: I know, but Harold, it's *Super Tech*!

HE: The last time we talked, didn't you say that you had just purchased a new computer? I remember you were excited about it.

DS: You know it! And I was right to be excited. It's been a terrific machine, does everything but make coffee—and I figure that's my fault 'cause I just don't know how to program it.

HE: Well, that's great. You were lucky to buy such a good toy.

DS: Lucky? Toy? Luck had nothing to do with it. I researched computers for weeks before I purchased that machine. Why, altogether, it cost almost $4,000! That's no toy.

HE: Okay, okay, I'm impressed. How *did* you decide that was the right one?

DS: First, I went through all of the back issues of my computer magazines for the last year. I subscribe to three. Then I bought a few computer-rating books. That helped me narrow it down to four possibilities. I checked them out at a few stores. Oh, wait, I remember now. I also called around to see who was using what. I eliminated one because a few of my friends told me the service was lousy. Then I went to the stores. I liked the look and feel of all three, so I took all of the tech material home, created a big spreadsheet, narrowed it down to two, called the dealers back to bargain for the best price, and bought my winner.

HE: I'm impressed. I'll bet you knew those machines inside out by the time you bought one.

DS: I think I could have built one.

HE: David, who's the president of Super Tech?

DS: What's that?

HE: Who's the president of Super Tech?

DS: How would *I* know?

HE: How big a piece of the U.S. PC market does Super Tech have and how does that compare to the share it had last year?

DS: What *are* you talking about? I have no earthly idea.

HE: How about Super Tech's price-to-book ratio or its price-to-earnings ratio? How do those figures compare to Lenovo's or Sony's?

DS: All I did was buy a home computer. What's that got to do with all these questions?

HE: Nothing.

DS: Nothing? Then what are you rambling on about?

HE: The $50,000 you want to plunk down on Super Tech. You've just finished eloquently describing what an amazingly intelligent, diligent process you went through to buy your computer, which is clearly not a toy. You put all that time and energy and work into a purchase that cost you almost $4,000, and now you expect me to take you seriously when you say you want to invest $50,000 in a company when you don't even know who the president is. Does that make any sense?

DS: Well, not if you put it that way; but I don't need to know all that stuff. All I need to know is that it's a good stock and the company's going places.

HE: Okay, let's talk about a good stock. Would you agree that a stock is good because it represents ownership in a good company?

DS: That makes sense.

HE: Is Super Tech a good company?

DS: Harold, that's a silly question. You know it is.

HE: I wouldn't argue with that. What's it selling for now?

DS: Right at $37.

HE: So Super Tech's a good company, you think it's a company on the move, and you can buy a share for about $37, right?

DS: That's right. And that's why I said it's a great stock and I want to buy it.

HE: David, suppose I told you that this morning's *Wall Street Journal* had a big write-up on Super Tech and described it in such glowing terms that today it's selling up $20 from yesterday, so it's trading at $57. Still want to buy it?

DS: I don't think I would. That's pretty expensive.

HE: Hold on. I didn't say Super Tech was in trouble. I said that the market experts agree with you and they think Super Tech's terrific. Why wouldn't you buy it?

DS: I told you. It would be too expensive at that price.

HE: Isn't Super Tech still a good company?

DS: Sure.

HE: Do you see the catch yet?

DS: No.

HE: It's simple. You fell into a classic Investor Trap. You've confused a good company with a good stock and a good price. When you raved about Super Tech and told me it was a great stock, you were talking about the company, not the stock. A company can be outstanding, but there is a price at which you just aren't getting what you pay for. The experts would say the stock is overpriced.

DS: Okay—

HE: The point is that in picking stocks, you've got to know two things and know them better than almost anyone else. 1) You have to know all about the company and how well it's likely to do in the future. 2) And you have to know what amount is a fair price to pay for a piece of that future. If you're still the expert in medicine that I've known you to be, you haven't had time to know that stock and its price better than anyone.

DS: That's pretty depressing. If that's true, how am I going to make money in the market?

HE: It's not that complicated. You spend your time finding and hiring the people who *do* have the time and brains to do the research. Why don't you come to our AAII 1 meeting next week? I'm going to be talking about the three Ps of selecting professional fund managers. My way won't make you rich, but it won't make you poor. If you want to get rich, do it by being a great doctor. The real market pros have little sympathy for novices. They just take their money.

DS: Okay, Harold. You've convinced me. I'm not buying. I'll see you next week at the AAII meeting. But you'd better have something good to say, because I'll still have that $50,000, and I want to put it to work for me.

HE: By the way, if you lost the money in your IRA, you can forget off-setting gains in your taxable accounts with the IRA loss. But if you make a killing with your IRA investment, that capital gain will eventually be taxed at the higher ordinary income rates. So whenever you see a real opportunity like Super Tech, let's talk about making the investment with your taxable money.

CHAPTER 2

THE TITANIC:

The Future Ain't What it Used to Be

We've seen the warning on every investment site, in every prospectus, in every description of every mutual fund ever peddled: "Past performance is not indicative of future returns." So it amazes me how many investors base their expectations for future investment returns on past market returns. Some base it on long-term historical returns because a long history seems to imply some statistical comfort. Others focus on more recent returns. Both approaches are recipes for disaster.

Bob: Hello, Harold.

Harold Evensky: Hi, Bob. We haven't talked in . . . gosh, let me check my watch. How have you and Mena been doing these last few days?

B: Harold, this is no time for small talk. I've been watching the markets.

HE: Like everybody else, I suppose. I can't seem to find a channel on television that isn't talking about the run-up in stocks.

B: Harold, it's taken me awhile to catch on but this is a great market!

HE: And that's what you called to tell me?

B: Look, I know I've been somewhat conservative about investing in the past.

HE: That may be an understatement. You think CDs are risky investments.

B: You never know when a bank is going to fail at just the moment when the FDIC fund is— Well, anyway, that's not why I called. I've been watching stocks go up and up and up, and I think I'm finally convinced that the stock market is where I need to put my retirement money.

HE: Let me have a look at your portfolio. Right now you have about 23.8 percent of your total assets in the stock market, and I remember having to twist your arm a few years ago to get you to go that high. So what kind of an increase are we talking about? Thirty percent? Thirty-two percent?

B: All of it.

HE: All of it? *You?* The fellow who remembers the Tech Bust and Grand Recession as if it were yesterday, wants to go all-in on stocks?

B: What's the problem? Stocks have been going up for the last five years. I know a trend when I see one.

HE: Bob, before you take this flying leap, could we talk for a minute? I'd like to get your advice on something that's been bothering me for a while. We can get back to your investment idea in a minute. Okay?

B: Sure.

HE: I've just finished reading a couple of economic studies by researchers for whom I have a lot of respect. They discuss the extraordinarily high market valuations based on price-to-earnings and price-to-book ratios in the markets today.

B: I think I know what those are. Price-to-earnings is called the P/E ratio. That's the stock price divided by the last twelve months' earnings and it tells you how expensive the stock is compared to what the firm is earning. Price-to-book is the P/B ratio and it's the company's stock price divided by the company's book value. It tells you how much you're paying per share for every dollar of company book value.

HE: That's good. A lot of investors would have no idea what those terms mean. Anyway, when you look at all these P/E and P/B ratios across the entire market, it looks as if stocks are very expensive compared to long-term values. —

B: So that means I've made a lot of money, and so have your other investors, right?

HE: I guess that's one way of looking at it. It's also yesterday's story. My challenge is that to calculate how much you and everybody else needs to save to have a reasonable probability of being able to afford retirement, I have to come up with an estimate of what kinds of returns you'll get in the future. We call it "future market return assumptions."

B: I don't understand why that's a problem. Can't you just base your projection on an average of what the markets have done in the past?

HE: I wish it were that predictable. Of course, I could do that. Unfortunately, there's no reason to believe that calculation would provide a reasonable "guesstimate" of future returns. I have to come up with a number I can believe in. When my clients are ready to retire some years down the road, having relied on that number, they need it to be right—or they can't retire.

B: Okay, so how can I help you?

HE: Tell me what you think about this: I look at today's valuations and the research, and everything tells me that the investment future cannot possibly be as rosy as it has been throughout the last couple of decades. So I'm sitting here at my desk telling myself that it's time to stop futzing around and acknowledge that, despite what financial headline writers seem to think, I believe they're being way too optimistic in estimating future market return assumptions. And I need to tell my clients that.

B: They're not going to like hearing that.

HE: Tell me about it. Why do you think I've put it off so long?

B: You *do* have a problem.

HE: I have to come up with a way to decide what numbers to plug into my fancy Monte Carlo software—and all the other sophisticated software I have on my desktop.

B: You know, Harold, maybe I'll wait a week or two while you look into this thing that's bothering you before I commit totally to the stock market. In fact, you know what you should do? Write an article about it. You're a good writer.

HE: I like that idea. I could call it "Heading for Disaster? The Assumptions Advisors Use for Investment Planning May Threaten Their Clients' Future."

B: Perfect title. And when you're finished with your research, we can revisit my portfolio.

HE: It's a deal.

[Two weeks later]

B: Hello, Harold.

HE: Hi, Bob. What's happening?

B: I was wondering if you've gotten around to writing that article yet. I noticed the market went up again yesterday, and I was thinking maybe I'm in danger of missing some of the upside of this bull market thing.

HE: Yes, your timing is perfect. I did write the article, and I submitted it yesterday. My research confirmed my gut feeling that the assumptions that I (and most practitioners) have been using for our planning are much too optimistic. I'm more convinced than ever that returns for many decades in the future could easily be significantly less than investors have enjoyed over the past seventy years.

B: So does that solve your problem?

HE: Not quite. Now I have to decide two things: What is the significance of lower returns for investors? And what should I do about it?

B: What have you concluded so far?

HE: That I still have more work to do, so I'm back to the drawing board. I've done some preliminary research and have an idea, but I need to give it some more thought. I've rearranged my schedule for the week so I'll have time to concentrate on this issue.

B: Sounds good. Mena and I will be taking a cruise soon so I'll touch base with you when we return.

HE: Have a great cruise and give me a call when you're back and catch your breath. We can then do some planning looking to the future and not the past.

Bob returns from his cruise in the next chapter and the story continues.

CHAPTER 3

NET, NET, NET:

—————◆—————

Expenses, Taxes and Inflation Can Eat Your Nest Egg – What To Do?

As dangerous as it is to simply extrapolate past returns into future expectations, an even bigger mistake is planning a financial future based on nominal gross returns, forgetting about how large a bite expenses, taxes, and inflation will take from the bottom line. Ultimately, all you truly have to spend is net-net-net returns—the amount left over after those three bullies have taken their share.

Bob: Hello, Harold.

Harold Evensky: Bob, how are you doing? How was the cruise?

B: It was terrific—pure decadence. We've already planned the next one. I had lots of time on the cruise and I've been thinking about our last conversation. I've decided that what you said seems pretty obviously true.

HE: What is? I'm eager to hear it, because lately it seems like nothing is obvious about investing.

B: That when I make investment decisions, I should be looking to the future, not to what happened yesterday.

HE: That's right, Bob. You've recognized one of the fundamental concepts of good investing. Planning your future through a rearview mirror is just as dangerous as using one to drive down a highway.

B: But now I have a problem. I like the idea of looking into the future, but I don't have a crystal ball, so I'm wondering if you've reached any conclusions regarding what to do in a world with lower returns.

HE: As I mentioned, I was feeling a little queasy myself when I started looking over the horizon and concluded that future returns are likely to be lower than we've seen in the past. As promised, while you were being spoiled on your cruise, I spent quite a bit of time thinking hard about what to do. In fact, I treated the question as if it were an engineering project. Engineering was my formal education—long, long ago.

B: So your engineering training came with a crystal ball?

HE: I dearly wish it had. For the last couple of weeks, I've been crunching numbers and running simulations. I actually put my thoughts and analysis into a paper that will be published in a professional journal. The title is "Changing Equity Premium Implications for Wealth Management Portfolio Design and Implementation." What do you think?

B: Very catchy. But I don't want to read an academic paper, especially not one with that title. I want to know what I should do.

HE: You're right. This isn't an academic exercise. We're talking about the quality of your life. But the answer actually isn't that complicated. We start with the idea that the markets aren't going to be handing out 12 percent-plus average yearly returns, even though this is what investors have come to expect from the stock market. I believe that future stock returns are likely to closer to 7½ percent and bonds about 3½ percent.

B: I'm with you so far, Harold. But be careful about throwing a lot of mathematics at me.

HE: So the question is: what will happen to your portfolio if you get lower returns in the future, right?

B: Right.

HE: Let's suppose a hypothetical investor is a little more adventurous than you are. He has 60 percent of his retirement money in stocks and 40 percent in bonds.

B: And he probably skydives on the weekend.

HE: Then we look at all the expenses. We take off a percent for the expense of managing the portfolio and assume an average tax rate of 20 percent, because the money is being managed carefully, since lots of the gain would be long-term capital gains, often deferred for many years.

B: Are those actual costs?

HE: They're actually lower than what a lot of people pay, but they're about right for somebody like you and the way we do things.

B: So what does that tell you?

HE: A simple math calculation shows that this brave investor might expect returns, after taxes and expenses, of around 5.9 percent a year. That's compared to more than twice that return for the prior five years.

B: Harold, those numbers are not as good as what I was hoping for when we talked about upping my stock exposure. You're basically assuming less than half the returns we've been getting. But I guess that's still better than zero returns or losing money.

HE: I agree. They're not great, but not catastrophic either. I wish that were the only bad news. But planner that I am, I realized I'd left out one major factor—inflation.

B: Okay. So what difference does inflation make?

HE: My last step was to calculate how much an investor could really count on. For all of us, that's what's left after paying expenses, Uncle Sam, and covering inflation—what I call net-net-net.

B: You sound depressed.

HE: The result almost put me in the hospital. It was only 2.9 percent!

B: Hold on a minute. You assume that returns on stocks drop from 14 percent to 7½ percent, but what I get to keep from my portfolio goes down 70 percent? Are you sure you weren't snoozing during the math classes when you studied engineering?

HE: No, I'm afraid my calculations aren't the problem. The problem is that in a low-return environment, returns go down, but expenses don't. So they start to represent a much bigger bite of total returns. An even bigger problem in a low-return environment is inflation. Although taxes are proportionate, inflation takes an even bigger bite, as it subsumes all returns, including the portion devoted to taxes and expenses.

B: So what do you do about that?

HE: You may not be able to control markets, but you *can* control taxes and expenses. So here's what I think we have to do: use an institutional portfolio design strategy known as core and satellite.

B: What's that? Investing in space travel?

HE: It just means you put most of your core stock investments into low-cost, tax-efficient index funds and ETFs that don't try to beat the market, which gets you market returns but at a very low cost. Our target is 80 percent of your stock investments in core investments.

B: I didn't know there were investments like that.

HE: There are quite a few. For example the iShare S&P 500 has an annual cost of less than one tenth of 1 percent compared to the average for a core, domestic, actively managed fund of 1½ percent plus. And because turnover is minimal, the fund is very tax efficient. In addition, ETFs, due to their design, may also provide additional tax benefits not available to mutual funds.

B: Are you trimming any other expenses?

HE: Since you're not trying to beat the market with your core investments, you don't have to do a lot of trading from one fund to another, which will keep transaction costs down as well as taxes. And if you believe that some active managers are capable of beating the market averages, which I do, you can concentrate all your active bets into the 20 percent of your stock investments allocated to a small number of actively managed funds. That's the portion of the portfolio I call the satellite.

B: Is there a bottom line to this?

HE: That's the really exciting part. I figure that by effectively managing taxes and investment expenses, you could save about ½ percent a year.

B: What?

HE: Check your e-mail; I just sent you a simple table showing how this all works out. It's actually beautiful.

B: So let me get this straight: the goal is to reduce my taxes and expenses by 1/2 percent a year?

HE: Yes. Are you as excited as I am?

B: I don't know how to tell you this, Harold, but that doesn't sound like much to me.

HE: If portfolios were churning out 14 percent a year, it *wouldn't* be much. But when we're talking about 2.9 percent a year, net-net-net, saving 1/2 percent by managing taxes and expenses for your portfolio means a 17 percent increase.

B: But what if you're wrong? What if the past twenty years are the way returns are going to be for the next twenty? *[See Chapter 12, "Pascal's Wager," for help in answering this question.]*

HE: That's a reasonable question. But it's important not to get caught up in probabilities, but to consider consequences as well. Based on today's valuations, I think the probability of lower returns is on my side. But if I'm wrong—and there is always that chance—then my strategy may reduce overall returns by maybe a percent, which is not a catastrophe if returns actually turn out to be high.

B: So, Harold—

HE: However, if I'm correct and we don't focus on managing taxes and expenses, your net-net-net return almost 20 percent lower. In retirement planning, that can make the difference between steak and cat food.

B: Harold—

HE: Basically, in this new environment, you need to chase tax and expense savings, not hot managers.

B: Harold?

HE: What.

B: Can we talk about my portfolio now?

HE: Of course. In fact, that's what we *are* talking about.

B: I'm starting to think that stocks may be riskier than I thought. You don't think there's a chance they could go down in value, do you?

HE: You mean, like, ever?

B: Yes.

HE: One of the few guarantees I'm prepared to make is that they will certainly go down in value at some point in the future, and some of those drops are going to be dramatic and scary. If I'm right, we may see more of them in the future than we have in the past.

B: So I should keep my money in CDs, right? Or do you think I should be more conservative than that?

HE: We've talked about confusing certainty with safety (*see Chapter 18*), and your response is a good example of it. I need to rerun your retirement projections in light of these more realistic numbers. When I do, it's possible I may conclude that with these lower return assumptions, you'll need *more* money in stocks, not less.

B: I don't follow you.

HE: With the returns you earned in the past, even that small allocation to stock was generating enough return to push your net worth up enough each year to keep you on track to meet your goals. But now you may need to take a little more market risk to get that same return.

B: I'm feeling queasy.

HE: Don't worry. It happens to all of us. But I'll be here to calm your nerves along the way.

CHAPTER 4

THE TROUBLE WITH SANDBOXES:

How to Tell if a Fund is All it Claims to Be

One of the hats I wear is as a Professor of Practice in the Personal Financial Planning Department at Texas Tech University where I teach the graduate Wealth Management class. Join me in class as I lecture on mutual funds.

There are thousands of mutual funds that offer to select stocks and bonds for your portfolio. But which ones are right for you?

Wealth Management Class: Good morning Professor Evensky,"

HE: Good morning, class. Are you ready to talk about the exciting topic of mutual fund selection?

[Enthusiastic cheers from the students sitting in the front row. The students sitting in the back look up from their smart phones.]

Can anybody tell me what the assignment was?

Michael: The assignment was to evaluate a particular mutual fund that's being promoted as the only stock fund you need for your portfolio.

Elizabeth: Professor Evensky, is this going to be on the test?

Clay: The ad read "It's the only domestic stock fund actively managed by professionals with performance that ranked it in the top 10 percent for the past one, three, five, ten, and fifteen years and below average risk."

HE: Thank you, Michael and Clay. So let's review some of the terms we're using here. Elizabeth, what is an actively managed fund?

Elizabeth: Hmm, sorry. I think I was out the day we covered that.

HE: Lisa?

Lisa: "Actively managed" refers to a fund where the manager actively trades the investments with the goal of outperforming an index return benchmark.

HE: And how is an actively managed fund different from an index fund?

Clay: Unlike the actively managed fund, an index manager makes no decisions about what stocks or bonds to buy. He simply wants to own all of the investments listed in the index. If the index drops a stock and adds a new one in its place, the index manager will sell the stock that was dropped and but the one that had been added to the index.

HE: So where did you start your evaluation? Anybody?

Cagla: I started with the three Ps: Philosophy, Process, and People, and I was impressed. Management seems to have a credible *philosophy*, a thoughtful *process*, and experienced *people*, although I noted that current management has only been in place about two and a half years. *[See Chapter 13, "The Three Ps of Investing," for more information.]*

HE: You're on a roll. Who's next?

Kristin: Well, having passed the three Ps, we then need to evaluate performance. Our clients can't get yesterday's returns, but if past performance is good and the fund passes the three Ps, our clients stand a chance of enjoying good performance in the future.

HE: Okay, how would you go about evaluating performance? And performance compared to what?

Lisa: I would begin by determining what sandbox the manager is playing in and select appropriate investable indexes to compare the fund to.

Elizabeth: Excuse me, um, "investable indexes"?

HE: Who can explain what an investable index is?

Lisa: It's a mutual fund or Exchange Traded Fund (they're called ETFs), available to public investors that have the goal of earning the return of a market index at low cost. For example: the iShares Core S&P 500 ETF seeks to track the results of the S&P 500 that measures the performance of large-capitalization stocks in the United States stock market. The annual fund cost is only 0.07 percent.

HE: Very good. Now, what's a "sandbox"? How are you going to determine which sandbox it is? And why investable indexes?

Lisa: By sandbox we mean the nature of the underlying investments. In this case, the fund is a domestic stock fund, so we need to determine the size of the companies the fund invests in and the manager's valuation orientation, so we can know the universe of managers to compare its performance to.

Elizabeth: "Valuation orientation"?

HE: Can someone explain valuation orientation? And tell us how we go about determining the universe for comparison.

Kristen: Generally stocks are categorized as "growth," "value," or "core." Growth companies are ones investors believe will have significantly improving profits. The stock price tends to be relatively high compared to the company's current earnings, as investors are paying up for those rapidly improving profits.

Value stocks tend to be relatively cheap based on current earnings, as investors do not have great expectations for the firm's future profits.

Core stocks are those that have mid-range expectations for future profits.

Professionals use a variety of metrics to determine what category a stock falls in. One of the most common is the stock's price-to-book ratio. That's simply a number that tells you how much you have to pay for a share of stock to buy $1 of the company's book value. For example, the stocks that make up the S&P 500 index have a price/book ratio of about 2.6 while the growth stock portion of that index is 3.8 and the value portion 1.9. When we look at a fund that's investing in S&P 500 kinds of stock, we'll look to see how the fund's P/B ratio compares. If it's in the 1.9 range then we consider it value, in the 2.8 range growth and core in between.

HE: Elizabeth, are you with us on this?

Elizabeth: Not really, sir.

HE: John, define average capitalization for us.

Kristin: Capitalization refers to the financial size of a company. It's calculated by multiplying the current price of a stock, times the number of shares of the company. So, for example, if a company has 100,000,000 shares outstanding and the stock is trading at $30 it would have a $3 billion capitalization. To give you an idea, the average of stocks in the S&P 500 is more than $60 billion. Although there is no hard and fast rule, generally we would consider stocks with capitalization of less than $2,000,000 small cap; between $2 and $5 billion mid-cap and more than $5 billion large cap.

HE: Okay. And why are we comparing the fund to investable indexes and not to an index?

Elizabeth: Professor Evensky, is that going to be on the test?

Clay: You taught us last week that an index is generally a more rigorous standard than a peer benchmark. But if our clients can't invest in an index, using one for comparison may be interesting but not very practical.

Sean: The good news is that today, with the large universe of exchange-traded fund index investments, we can invest in almost any index.

Elizabeth: I don't seem to have any notes on exchange-traded funds.

HE: Very good. Sean, where might we look for the information we need to evaluate funds?

Sean: Certainly we'd want to look at the fund family website, and to get an independent evaluation, we'd look to Morningstar data. It is available in programs for professionals and on the Web for retail investors. You told us Morningstar is the Rolls Royce of the profession.

HE: Okay. What's next in our evaluation? And what did you find?

Sean: I found the price-to-book and capitalization to be in line with the mid-cap growth universe. For comparison, I selected two exchange-traded funds (ETFs): iShare S&P mid-cap growth and iShare Russell mid-cap growth. Besides the capitalization and price-to-book metrics being similar to the active fund, the correlations with both indexes were high at 0.94.

HE: Thank you, Sean. And?

Kristin: Regarding performance, I found that during its ten-year-plus history, the fund's return compared to the indexes was most impressive; it was almost 20 percent better than the index returns.

HE: So it does stand apart, so to speak? What do you think, Linda?

Linda: Not so fast is what I think. When I looked more closely, I found that all of that 20 percent outperformance was attributable to returns more than five years ago. When I looked at the most recent last three years, when current management was in place, I found that all the outperformance disappeared.

HE: Terrific. Kiran, what did you find?

Kiran: I looked at tax efficiency.

HE: And?

Kiran: Throughout the last three years, there was almost a 1 percent extra tax drag on the active fund as compared to the much more tax-efficient index funds.

HE: Conclusions?

Kiran: My conclusion would be that, while the fund seems to be of decent quality, if I were making a recommendation to my client, I would recommend the exchange-traded fund.

HE: And why is that?

Kiran: Recent performance of all three funds was quite close on a pretax basis; however, on an after-tax basis the index alternatives would deliver more after tax returns to my taxable clients. Also, with an index investment, I'm basically sure of par performance; that is, after expenses an index will consistently be in the top half of the performance universe, whereas an active manager may do well for one period but poorly the next. So, unless I find an active manager I believe can consistently outperform an index alternative, I'll stick with the index. It's like going out on the golf course and being guaranteed to shoot par.

HE: And the moral?

Kristin: Next time I read a glowing article about a hot shot manager, I won't add that manager to my clients' portfolios until I determine what sandbox the manager's playing in, put him through the screen of the three Ps, and select an investable benchmark to compare his risk and returns to. And if it's for a taxable account, I won't forget to consider taxes.

Elizabeth: Professor Evensky, is this going to be on the test?

HE: Think of this as a very tough life test, Elizabeth, one that every investor has to pass more than once on the road to retirement.

CHAPTER 5

BIGGEST MISTAKE:

———◆———

A Great Stock and a Great Investment May Not Be the Same

"That's a great stock; I think I'll take a big position in my portfolio." That's how all too many investors make their investment decisions. Mistake, *big* mistake.

Randi: Hello, Harold.

Harold Evensky: Hi, Randi. What's new in the accounting world?

R: Don't ask. It seems like every time Congress passes a law simplifying the tax code, they add a thousand more pages to it.

HE: So what are you calling about? Do you want me to flex my lobbying muscles?

R: Actually, it has to do with the newsletter I edit for our professional accounting group. It's our investment issue, and I can't think of anyone more qualified to help me with it.

HE: I'm flattered. How can I help?

R: The issue coming up is a very important one. I was wondering if you could give me a great topic for the lead article.

HE: Now I'm even *more* flattered. How about a story on the biggest investment mistake most investors make?

R: What a great idea! You're so smart!

HE: Well, shucks, I was hoping somebody would notice.

R: With all your investment wisdom, what mistake do you think the article should discuss?

HE: Well, where should I start? Investors had been making the biggest mistake for a long time, but it wasn't until August 1991 that advisors started to give it serious consideration.

R: What happened in 1991—other than a new tax law?

HE: That month, a prestigious investment journal published an article that would eventually turn the investment profession upside down.

R: I knew you were the right person to call.

HE: It carried the fancy title "Determination of Portfolio Performance." The authors—three big-time money managers named Gary Brinson, Paul Hood, and Gil Beebower—thought it might be a good idea to study the importance of various decisions made every day in managing huge, billion-dollar pension portfolios.

R: Are you telling me that nobody before that had been thinking about whether they were making good or bad decisions?

HE: They were the first to look at the types of decisions in a systematic way. They started by deciding what decisions were actually being made.

R: Like which stocks to buy?

HE: They divided the types of decisions made into categories, and that was one of them. They decided there were only three kinds of decisions that anyone could make that would affect a portfolio's performance.

R: And one of them is which stocks to buy?

HE: Yes. They called it security selection, which means picking the best stocks and bonds or the best managers.

R: What were the other two decisions?

HE: I'm sure you've heard of the second one. They called it market timing. Basically, that means deciding when to be in or out of the market. If the market is going to go down, you want to be on the sidelines. If it's going up, you want to be totally invested in it.

R: Doesn't that require predicting the future?

HE: Believe it or not, some professionals, and many retail investors, think they can predict where the stock market will go up or down. So this was the second of their basic decision categories.

R: And the last one?

HE: That one was the real insight. Even before picking the best stocks and bonds, you have to decide how much to put in stocks and how much to put in bonds. This is sometimes referred to as the asset allocation decision. In the article, it was called the investment policy.

R: And those are the only kinds of decisions you make when you invest?

HE: If you can come up with a significant fourth decision, you may be in line for a Nobel Prize.

R: All right. So how do you decide—how did you put it—the importance of each of these decisions?

HE: The researchers decided to look at the decisions and at the performance data of many sophisticated managers over time. And did they ever! The final study used ten years' worth of data from ninety-one big-time pension plans ranging in size from $700 million to $3 billion in assets. This represented a significant percentage of professionally managed pension money in the United States, managed by some of the nation's top money managers.

R: Wait. Let me write that down. Okay, so did they find anything noteworthy?

HE: When they looked at their results the authors observed that the results are striking. Startling might have been an even more accurate adjective.

R: What was so startling?

HE: First, they found that two of the types of decisions were actually, in aggregate over the total sample, subtracting returns.

R: Wait a minute. Say that again.

HE: That's what was so startling. They were looking at the performance generated by the brains and talent of many of the best and brightest of the nation's portfolio managers to: first, pick the very best stocks and bonds for the portfolios they were managing, and second, to time their trading to try to be in when the markets were going up and out when the markets were going down. And guess what?

R: What?

HE: Looking at all those decisions and the effects of all those decisions, it turns out that on average they contributed negative performance. With all that brainpower and knowledge and experience, the returns were reduced.

R: But that doesn't make any sense. What about that third category of decisions? The investment policy thing?

HE: Their most important conclusion was that more than 93 percent of the variation in portfolio returns was attributable to policy—meaning, to the mix of assets that they selected.

R: So if I get the mix of stocks and bonds and foreign stocks and all the other assets right, that's way more important than trying to pick which stocks are going to outperform other ones?

HE: You're catching on much faster than people in my profession did. It took years for the people in investment management to buy into this conclusion and realize what it meant. So I think you've gotten the core of what you need for the article. I'll send you a copy of the Brinson-Hood-Beebower study and their follow-up study, which came to almost exactly the same conclusions.

R: Can you talk with me about this just a little longer? I feel as if I'm basking in the sunshine of your wisdom.

HE: Really? Well, you know, I guess I'm not quite as busy as I thought. But what else is there to say?

R: I just need to know how this relates to that biggest mistake thing you were talking about.

HE: Let me give you a hint. Do you know what your investment policy is?

R: Mine? Now that you mention it, no. I don't think I have one.

HE: No investor can avoid having an investment policy. You have one now, but you have it by default.

R: That doesn't sound good. So how do I find out what mine is?

HE: It's not hard to figure out at all. In fact, let's keep it as simple as possible. Take out a pad and make two columns. Write down how much you have in your money market funds, your bond funds, both in personal accounts, your IRA, and 401(k), and how much money you have in stock funds, again, in your personal account, IRA, and 401(k). For now, just make estimates, okay?

R: All right, I'm just writing down some numbers here. Let's say I have $12,000 in a money market fund, $28,000 in a bond fund in a taxable account, and $15,000 in bond funds in my 401(k). Then there's $30,000 in stock funds in a taxable account and $15,000 in stock funds in my IRA.

HE: Fine. Now we can translate that into percentages pretty easily, just by calculating the percent of the total. You have a total of 55 percent of your money in cash and bonds and 45 percent in stocks and growth investments. Therefore, the policy is 55 percent cash/bonds and 45 percent stock.

R: And that's my big mistake?

HE: The biggest mistake is having an investment policy designed by accident. Think about it. Do you really want 90+ percent of your financial future determined by chance?

R: No. But does that breakdown really determine more than 90 percent of my future returns?

HE: Not necessarily; 90 percent might be overstating it, but most professional advisors would agree that not carefully deciding how to allocate your investments among cash, bonds, and stocks is a *big* mistake. If you can't explain why your portfolio investment allocation looks like the one you have, it's time for you to do some serious thinking about your investments and redesign your policy.

R: How do I know when I have an appropriate policy?

HE: You'll know you're done and you can explain just why your portfolio is divvied up as it is.

R: Perfect. I'm done.

HE: Done with what?

R: The article you just dictated to me. I have it pretty much written, and I didn't even have to do any research. I'll meet my deadline and I won't even have to stay up late.

HE: Just—you know—for the sake of argument, when was your deadline?

R: Tomorrow morning. Why do you think I called a smart guy like you?

HE: I've been had, haven't I?

R: Good-bye, Harold. I have a lot of work to do, so I don't have a lot of time to chat. I'll call you when I start working on our next issue.

CHAPTER 6

GETTING YOUR MONEY:

———◆———

The Difference Between Liquidity and Marketability

Having the option to sell an investment whenever you want and getting *all* of your money back is not the same thing.

Dr. Elizabeth Boone is a surgeon, a long-time friend and client. I'd been looking forward to chatting with Elizabeth about how my alma mater just trounced hers in basketball.

Receptionist: Hello, Harold; it's Dr. Boone on 88.

HE: Hello, Elizabeth. Did you see the game?

EB: Forget it, Harold. Our best rebounder was out with a broken collarbone, the referees had to use braille to read the scoreboard, and our coach had the flu. Besides, I've got a problem.

HE: Sorry, Elizabeth. What's up?

EB: I need some advice for my mom.

HE: About?

EB: She just received an inheritance from my aunt's estate and she's asking me how to invest it. I told her CDs are safe, but right now the rates are so low that she'd get more return if she buried her money in the backyard.

She doesn't have to pay much in the way of taxes and since she mostly needs income, her broker suggested one of those government bond funds and preferred stock that pay high dividends. I wanted to check with you to make sure that was all right.

HE: Good grief!

EB: Excuse me?

HE: Elizabeth, I've heard this same story about six zillion times. Let me ask you a few questions: first, how worried would your mom be about principal fluctuation?

EB: What on earth does principal fluctuation mean?

HE: Will your mom be worried if the value of her fund goes up and down, as long as her income is fairly steady?

EB: I don't even need to ask her. She and Dad had big tax-free bond portfolio years ago. When interest rates went up, they'd watch their bond prices go down with each statement! I thought they'd die from bleeding ulcers. Harold, I also had lots of those long-term bonds and I still have the ulcers. Never again! You know how I feel about that. You're the one who restructured my portfolio.

HE: Okay, Elizabeth, okay. Just checking. Second question: how carefully have you or your mom checked into the suggestion of government funds and preferreds?

EB: Pretty well, Harold. You know my mom—she's sharp. She asked a lot of good questions of the broker and jotted down the answers. Let me read you the gist of how the conversation went:

Broker: Mrs. E., based on what you've said, you want income and safety, right?

Mrs. E.: Right.

Broker: Well, I think we should split your investment between our government fund and a portfolio of well-selected preferred utility stocks.

Mrs. E.: Mr. Broker, this is almost all of my money and you're right, I'm really concerned about safety and income. How safe are these investments?

Broker: Mrs. E., the preferred stocks we'll buy are all from highly rated companies—real blue chips—and the government fund invests in bonds guaranteed by the United States government. We're talking *safety*!

Mrs. E.: What happens if I need my money?

Broker: Why, Mrs. E., don't you worry, there are safe investments.

HE: That's it? That was their conversation?

EB: Mom also said he was really comforting. He even got up from his desk and walked over and patted her shoulder and said, "These investments are exceptionally safe and you can sell whenever you want. Just call me and I'll put in an order and you'll have your money in a week." Then he said, "Now, if you'll just sign here—"

HE: But she didn't sign, right? Tell me she didn't sign and I'll be a lot happier.

EB: Mom told the broker she wanted to talk to me first. She asked him to mail some information and I have it now.

HE: Let me guess. The prospectus on the government fund says "guaranteed by the federal government." And the brochure has American flags all over it.

EB: You know this fund?

HE: No, but I do recognize the marketing strategy. And the rating sheets for the preferred stocks he wants her to buy say that the company balance sheets are so strong they could win an Olympic weight-lifting championship.

EB: Something like that. So we should go ahead? I started to tell her to go ahead, but remembering those great tickets I got you to the big game, I figured you owed me a bit of free advice.

HE: Elizabeth, I'll give you the free advice, and I won't even mention the current price of the other four hot tips I talked you out of.

EB: Touché! So what's your diagnosis?

HE: I don't think you want me to give you a lecture on good financial planning. Suffice it to say your mom shouldn't do anything but put the money into a money market account until she reviews her entire financial situation, including her needs for cash flow and emergency reserves, tax planning, insurance, and her estate planning as well as her Social Security and pension income. All of those will make a difference in deciding what she should buy.

EB: All that?

HE: When you do a diagnosis, do you just give advice off the cuff based on what the patient says she wants, or do you probe a little bit?

EB: I probe a lot. What kind of a doctor do you think I am?

HE: A good one. So you can see my point. But if you want me to diagnose your mom from afar, then let me at least introduce you to two important ideas that will help you evaluate the investments Mr. Broker suggested: liquidity and marketability—the big *L* and *M*.

EB: I need to write this down so I can tell Mom.

HE: Don't get hung up on the fancy words—focus on the concepts. Both liquidity and marketability refer to attributes of investments. You've heard me say that investments don't have morals; they're not good or bad. They have attributes, and those might be right or wrong for you or your mom, just as an antibiotic might be good for a patient with an infection but not so good for helping a patient who's in a lot of pain.

EB: Maybe you should leave the medical analogies to me.

HE: Liquidity measures how easily your investment can be converted into cash whenever you want to, no matter what's happening in the economy or to the stock or bond market, *without losing any of your original investment.* Marketability measures how easy it is to sell an investment when you want to. With me so far?

EB: I'm not sure. Those sound the same.

HE: You're right; they do. Both relate to converting your investment to cash. Both measure how fast and how easy it is to do that. And neither is good nor bad. The problem is that they're not the same.

EB: So tell me how they're different.

HE: There's one *big* difference. Liquidity refers to getting the *full amount* of your original investment back at any time. Marketability is about getting *fair market value* when you sell. And there's the catch! You know yourself from your ulcer experiences with the bond funds that *full amount* and *fair market value* are often *very* different.

EB: So if the market goes down, and Mom tells the broker she wants her money back—

HE: The amount she gets could be less than she invested originally. And she's back on ulcer medicine—or worse. She could be in danger of running out of money.

EB: So she wants something liquid, right? What kinds of investments are liquid?

HE: The most common liquid investments are checking and savings accounts, money market funds, Treasury bills, and that wad of cash she was going to bury in the backyard.

EB: And marketable investments are?

HE: There are lots of marketable investments. The list includes stocks and bonds, mutual funds, and government bond funds. Got it now?

EB: I think so, but so what?

HE: So knowing what you know now, take another look at that government fund with the flags on the brochure and the preferreds with their balance sheets on steroids. Suppose your mom wanted to sell her government fund or preferred in a few years. How much would she get back?

EB: I guess I really don't know. How could I?

HE: You can't unless you have a working crystal ball. You don't have one, do you?

EB: No.

HE: I always ask, because I hope that one day I'll find someone who has one and I can ask to borrow it for a while.

So we know the government fund is secure from a credit standpoint, and for now let's assume the preferred stock issuers remain in good financial shape. But with both investments, you still have interest rate risk. That's what the broker should have talked about, and probably would have, if he or she wasn't so focused on making the sale.

EB: You mean the risk that interest rates will go up?

HE: Exactly. The broker is selling your mom two investments paying a fixed interest rate. Right?

EB: Right.

HE: When interest rates go up, people can go out on the market and buy investments with fixed rates higher than what you mom is getting. So do you think anybody would want to buy her investment, with a lower yield, at the price she paid for it?

EB: No.

HE: You're right. To take an extreme example, let's say she buys a bond with a twenty-year maturity today and gets a fixed 4 percent, and ten years from now, interest rates have gone up to the point where a bond with the same credit rating, and ten years to maturity, by the same issuer, is paying 8 percent. If she wanted to sell her bonds, she would be offered about $7,000 for her $10,000 investment. She'd lose money and get an ulcer.

EB: Okay, but she still has the preferred stocks, right?

HE: Let's talk about those. From the talk about interest rate risk, you can see that the longer the maturity of the investment, the more interest rate risk you're taking. Rates probably aren't going to double in one year, but they just might in ten. And during twenty years, you have no idea what's going to happen, right?

EB: Right.

HE: So tell me: what is the maturity date on the preferred stocks the broker was recommending?

EB: I don't know. Ten years?

HE: What if I told you it was thirty? Would you be comfortable then?

EB: Not very, no.

HE: What if I told you it was 100?

EB: That would make me extremely uncomfortable.

HE: And if I said that those investments would mature in a thousand years, what would you say to me?

EB: I'd say you were joking.

HE: Actually, I was underestimating. The answer is that those preferred stock investments never mature.

EB: Never?

HE: Not even when the Earth crashes into the sun. So your mom is subject to a seriously whopping interest rate risk. And it gets worse.

EB: How can it possibly?

HE: If you own a bond issued by the company selling the preferred stock and the company fails to pay on its bond obligation, it files bankruptcy. Guess what that same company does if it can't pay on your preferred stock?

EB: What?

HE: It sends an apology letter.

EB: So maybe the broker's advice wasn't as great as I thought it was. Mom says he was really nice.

HE: I'm sure he's a very nice person who pets his dog. But the bottom line for your mom is that those government bond funds and preferreds may have a good story, and they pay what today seems like an attractive rate, but they come with a boatload of risks and they are, irrevocably, not liquid. They certainly may play a role in many portfolios but not 100 percent of your moms.

EB: So what do I do? What would you recommend?

HE: First, let me ask: why didn't your mom buy CDs?

EB: I told you. Those one- and two-year CDs just don't pay enough.

HE: Did you look at the five-year CDs?

EB: Actually, we did. They were a little more attractive, but mom's afraid to buy anything locked up for more than a few days.

HE: Elizabeth, that's exactly the point! She was confusing liquidity with marketability.

EB: Yet again, I don't follow you.

HE: It's not that complicated. Tell me: if your mom purchased a five-year CD today and in three years she needed her money, what would happen?

EB: Actually, we asked about that. They said if we liquidated early, they would charge a six-month interest penalty.

HE: And that means?

EB: Mom would get her investment back and a little less interest than she had expected.

HE: Right; she would get *her entire initial investment back* and maybe even a little interest. Sounds like a liquid investment. Not very locked up, is it?

EB: Not when you put it that way.

HE: Your mom needs to be sure not to be misled by marketing that confuses liquidity with marketability. "Getting your money back" isn't the same as getting *all* of your money back.

EB: Okay, I'll talk to her.

HE: Maybe she can come to the game with us.

EB: What game?

HE: The game you're going to get me tickets to, the one where your leading rebounder is going to be out, and our coaching staff has checked with the local institute for the blind to bring in some qualified referees.

EB: I'll see what I can scare up. Thanks, Harold.

HE: I'm glad I could help.

CHAPTER 7

FALSE SECURITY:

———◆———

When Stop Loss May Really Mean
Guaranteed Loss

I was reading a story in one of my profession's trade journals about a financial advisor's solution to helping retired clients develop income strategies in a volatile market. The advisor has been in business since the early 1970s, but the 2008 financial crisis was his wake-up call to move to "tactical investing."

I have to confess that I'm a skeptic about anyone's ability to call market turns, so I was already biased when I started reading the article. But I lost it when the story said his major strategy was using stop-loss orders to avoid big declines.

For those not familiar with a stop-loss order, I'll explain: it's an instruction to your broker to put in a sell order if your stock price ever drops below a predetermined price.

To find out more about the dangers of this strategy, let's eavesdrop on this advisor's conversation with a customer.

Dr. Charles (Dr. C.): Hello, Joe [the broker]. This is Dr. Charles.

Broker: Dr. Charles, how can I protect your investments today?

Dr. C: I have a large investment in High Tech, Inc., after all, you recommended it to me.

B: A terrific investment recommendation, if I may say so myself.

Dr. C.: Well, yes, but the thing is I'm becoming a bit concerned about it.

B: Why? High Tech is the future.

Dr. C.: Maybe so, but the stock is bouncing around like a yo-yo. It's finally back up over the high it reached eighteen months ago, but I'm afraid, given its history, it's going to drop back down again on me.

B: Would you like me to protect you from your stock investments going down?

Dr. C.: Exactly! Would you?

B: Certainly. I've been practicing this safe investment methodology since, well—there really isn't any reason to get into how recently I've changed my entire investment philosophy. The point is it looks as if you need a stop-loss order.

Dr. C.: A stop-loss order? Is that what it sounds like it is?

B: The point of a stop loss is to stop your losses and let you keep your gains. You like gains, don't you?

Dr. C.: Yes. Yes, I do.

B: And what about losses?

Dr. C.: Not so much.

B: So let's look at the old terminal here. I see that High Tech is trading at about $56½, which is a pretty nice run during the past couple of weeks.

Dr. C.: Right. But before that run, it was priced below what I paid for it.

B: It looks like the last trade was at $56. It's been trading in a pretty narrow range, between $50 and $60, for the last few days.

Dr. C.: So what can I do to protect myself from the next drop?

B: Tell you what. I'll put a stop loss in for you at $52. Your basis is $48 so, if worse comes to worst, you'll lock in a profit of $4/share.

Dr. C.: Thank you, Joe. You're the best. Now I can sleep at night.

[Nine months later]

Dr. C.: Hello, Joe.

B: Hello, Dr. Charles. How can I protect your investments today?

Dr. C.: Well, you may have noticed the screaming headlines in the newspapers or heard the cable television folks talking about the fact that the bottom dropped out of the tech market.

B: I did notice, yes.

Dr. C.: High Tech was clobbered worse than most. I just wanted to be sure my stop loss got executed.

B: Yes, sir, I see your position now. It did get traded.

Dr. C.: Thank goodness, I just saw it trading at $32! Sure am glad I got out at $48. With my 10,000 shares, I still made a nice profit of $40,000. Thanks, Joe. That's all I wanted to find out.

B: Uh, hold on a minute. You're correct that it's now trading at $32.25. But when the initial sell-off hit, the stock actually dropped all the way down to $27.

Dr. C.: Now, I feel even better that I was able to sell out.

B: Well, that's the thing. When your stock dropped below $48, that triggered your stop-loss order, all right. Then your shares were sold at market. Unfortunately, the price you sold at was $29.50 not $48.

Dr. C.: What?! How could you have sold me out at $29.5?! I said I wanted $48 minimum.

B: Well, I'm afraid that's not how a stop-loss order works. I just assumed you knew that when we set it up. All a stop loss does is trigger an open-sell order when and if the stock price drops below the stop-loss price. What happened with High Tech is that with the huge volume of sell orders pouring in, a few trades were done at $48, resulting in your open order to sell "at market." Unfortunately, there was already a ton of sell orders on the books ahead of you. So by the time your order was executed, the price was $29.50.

[One week later]

Dr. C.: Hello, Harold.

Harold Evensky (HE): Pardon me. Who is this?

Dr. C.: My name is Dr. Charles. I saw you were quoted in the *Journal*, and you had some skeptical things to say about stop-loss orders. I'm looking for a new financial advisor, and I was hoping you could tell me more about what you think of stop-loss strategies.

HE: On the surface, they look great. They cost nothing, and they preserve all the possibility of further gains, and if you don't know how they work, you might think that they eliminate the potential of loss beyond the stop-loss order price. Unfortunately, that's an illusion.

Dr. C.: Tell me more.

HE: The major problem with stop-loss orders is they're executed mindlessly. There is no guarantee what price you'll sell at once the stop-loss order is triggered. If the market's falling rapidly, you may end up selling at a price well below your stop-loss price.

Dr. C.: Actually, I found that out the hard way.

HE: I'm sorry to hear that. But you're not alone. Here's a quote from John Gabriel, a Morningstar strategist:

One type of trade that we vehemently avoid more than any other is known as a "stop-loss" order. Consider yourself warned: if you perform an online search for this term, you're likely to find some misleading definitions. For instance, you may come across an explanation like, "setting a stop-loss order for 10 percent below the price you paid for the security will limit your loss to 10 percent." *Our main problems with this statement are that it is bla-tantly false, imparts a false sense of security, and can lead to truly disastrous results.*

Dr. C.: I wish I'd seen that a month ago.

HE: Gabriel went on to say, "We often quip that a more appropriate name for a stop-loss order would be a guaranteed-loss order"—strong stuff and I couldn't agree more.

Dr. C.: Do you know of any strategy that does work to limit losses?

HE: You can somewhat mitigate the risk of selling way below your tar-geted stop-loss price by using what's called a stop-loss limit order. It's a little more complicated, but it tells your broker to enter a sell order if the price drops below the stop-loss, but also tells him not to sell if it falls below an even lower limit order. The catch is, if that happens, it means you still own the stock after the price has dropped.

Dr. C.: So, in other words, safety is an illusion.

HE: My bottom line is: If you decide to be a market maven and pick your own stock, then you should decide when to sell, depending on the market environment at the time. Don't fall for the false security of a mind-less automatic trigger. In fact, you may not want to sell at all.

Dr. C.: What do you mean?

HE: When you go to the grocery store and something goes on sale and the price is really cheap, does that mean you go home, rummage around your refrigerator, and offer to sell stuff back to the store at a price that is lower than you bought it?

Dr. C.: Of course, not. I'd probably take advantage of the low price and buy extra.

HE: Then why do people do just the opposite with stocks? When stocks go on sale, the first thing people think about is selling. To my way of thinking, a big drop in price may be a terrific opportunity to buy more, not a reason to sell.

Dr. C.: I never thought of that.

HE: If you want to come in and talk with me, I can set up an appointment. But I'm going to warn you in advance: I don't have any magic formula for protecting you against the ups and downs of the stock market.

Dr. C.: Believe it or not, at the moment, that's music to my ears.

CHAPTER 8

UMBRELLAS AND BUMBERSHOOTS:

How Risky Investments Can Make for a Safer Portfolio

Harold Evensky: Good morning, class.

Class: Good morning, Professor Evensky.

Andrew: Professor Evensky, why are you carrying that umbrella? The temperature outside is 110 degrees and it hasn't rained in the past three months!

HE: Andrew, that's an excellent question. And this umbrella is what we call a prop. It will help introduce one of the most important issues in wealth management: diversification and asset allocation, and why they're so important in helping our clients meet their goals.

Elizabeth: Professor Evensky, will this be on the test?

HE: So I've prepared a little exercise to help all of us think through how to make investment recommendations in light of client goals. Is everybody ready?

Class: Yes.

HE: In this exercise, our clients live in a simple world where they have a choice of only three investments. Two of them are risky. I'll write the choices here on the whiteboard:

Investment Alternatives		
Investment		**Return**
CD		8 percent
Swimsuit company stock	If it's sunny	20 percent
	If it's not sunny	0 percent
Umbrella company stock	If it's sunny	0 percent
	If it's not sunny	20 percent

HE: Everybody got that? As a sophisticated planner, you recognize that the swimsuit and umbrella company stocks are very risky, since an investor will either make a great return or no return, depending on the weather. So you've consulted with some of the world's greatest meteorologists and arrived at the following:

METEOROLOGISTS' PREDICTIONS

80 percent probability that it will be rainy 90 percent of the time

60 percent probability that it will be rainy 70 percent of the time

30 percent probability that it will be rainy only 20 percent of the time

How would you recommend my clients allocate their investments? Where do you start?

Andrew: Well, you say we should always start with what we know about our clients.

HE: Great start, Andrew. And what important things do we know about them?

Andrew: To achieve their goals, they need at least a 10 percent return. We also know they are not very tolerant of investment volatility. They don't like their investments to bounce around a lot.

HE: Good so far. Kiran, where does that take us?

Kiran: Only now should we look at the investments. We should look at the possible investment outcomes—which, in this case, seem to depend on the weather.

Nicholas: Professor Evensky, while everybody else was chattering on about the clients, I made up a little table that shows all the different possible portfolio returns based on the weather data you gave us.

HE: Thank you, Nicholas.

Nicholas: I also created a neat little algorithm that will do these same calculations if we ever run into a problem like this again. I could show you after class.

HE: Nicholas, I'm going to go out on a limb and predict that you have a bright future as an investment analyst.

Nicholas: Whatever. Wait. That doesn't mean I'll have to talk to actual people, does it?

Carly: Professor Evensky, I'll check Nicholas's math.

PORTOFLIO RETURNS BASED ON POSSIBLE WEATHER OUTCOMES

SUN FREQUENCY	UMBRELLA INVESTMENT									
	100	90	80	70	60	50	40	30	20	10
0	20%	18%	16%	14%	12%	10%	8%	6%	4%	2%
10	18%	20%	18%	16%	14%	12%	10%	8%	6%	4%
20	16%	18%	20%	18%	16%	14%	12%	10%	8%	6%
30	14%	16%	18%	20%	18%	16%	14%	12%	10%	8%
40	12%	14%	16%	18%	20%	18%	16%	14%	12%	10%
50	10%	12%	14%	16%	18%	20%	18%	16%	14%	12%
60	8%	10%	12%	14%	16%	18%	20%	18%	16%	14%
70	6%	8%	10%	12%	14%	16%	18%	20%	18%	16%
80	4%	6%	8%	10%	12%	14%	16%	18%	20%	18%
90	2%	4%	6%	8%	10%	12%	14%	16%	18%	20%
100	0%	2%	4%	6%	8%	10%	12%	14%	16%	18%

HE: Thank you, Carly. So does everybody see where the numbers come from?

Suppose, for example, you have 90 percent allocated to umbrellas and it rains 70 percent of the time. That means you will profit from all of the 70 percent rainy days. That's a net of 14 percent to 20 percent, maximum, times 70 percent, right, Nicholas?

Nicholas: Obviously.

HE: Okay, now let's consider how we did with our swimsuit company investment. Since only 10 percent is invested in the swimsuit company, and there are 30 percent sunny days, the swimsuit company can profit from only some of those sunny days. So my return is 20 percent, maximum, times the 10 percent I have invested in swimsuits, which equals 2 percent. Add 2 percent return from swimsuits to 14 percent return from umbrellas, and you get a total of 16 percent. If this turns out to be the real weather pattern, I didn't get the full 20 percent because I owned too many umbrellas and not enough swimsuits.

Kiran: And that's where all the other possibilities came from?

HE: Correct. You can use the same process to calculate the other figures in the chart. So now what? Do you have an answer to the proper allocation for these clients who need 10 percent a year and don't like a lot of volatility?

Alicia: Well, I guess we have to toss out the safe investment.

HE: Good, Alicia. Why?

Alicia: At a fixed 8 percent, the CD is a nonstarter. For someone who needs 10 percent, only receiving 8 percent, no matter how guaranteed, would be a failure.

HE: Good thinking. Of course, when you present the alternatives, our client might elect to revise the goals so that 8 percent would suffice. But before we recommend that, let's look at the risky alternatives. What do you see here?

Kiran: I'd apply Modern Portfolio Theory, and come up with a blend of the risky investments. If you blend investments that respond differently to different investment climates, then the result is a portfolio with less volatility.

HE: Very good. And did y'all get my joke? Investment climate—rain or sun—pretty funny, right?

Kiran: Professor Evensky, maybe you shouldn't try to be funny in class.

HE: Yes, well, the important thing is that we can blend these risky investments. And in this simplified investment world we've created, what do you notice immediately?

Alicia: The risk and return patterns are exactly the opposite. You make money in swimsuits when it's sunny, and when it rains, your return comes from umbrellas. It either rains or it doesn't.

HE: Right. So?

Alicia: So in that simplified investment world, if we put half in swimsuits and half in umbrellas, we'd always be making 20 percent on half of our portfolio and 0 percent on the other half.

HE: And?

Andrew: For these clients, if they invest half of their money in swimsuits and half in umbrellas, no matter what happens, even if it never rains again or the deluge never ends, or anything in between, the clients will get a guaranteed 10 percent return—which is exactly what the client needs.

HE: Excellent. Of course, in the real world, you probably have thousands of different drivers of the profits of tens of thousands of different companies. If you were to bet on any one of them, there's the possibility that whatever you were betting on, just the opposite would happen and you could lose a lot of money. But if you spread your bets around, and the economy grows—which it has done since people were living in caves—then all of those bets across all of those different drivers will smooth out some of the ups and downs. And there's a high probability, based on history, that your clients will get returns commensurate with their willingness to wade into the world of market risk. Diversification really works.

Kiran: But there's still risk, right?

HE: Of course. The moral here is not that you can eliminate risk; but in designing your portfolio and evaluating risk, you need to consider the risk of the combined investments, not the risk of each individual investment. And let's not miss something equally important: you need to consider the risk of not achieving your goals by confusing certainty and safety. Does everybody get it?

Class: Yes, Professor Evensky.

HE: And yes, Elizabeth, this *will* be on the test.

Elizabeth: What's that?

HE: But I wanted to get back to something we talked about earlier. Who thought that my investment climate joke was funny? And try to keep in mind that your grade might depend on it.

PART 2:

ALL ABOUT PLANNING AND ADVICE

CHAPTER 9

ADVISORS:

———————————◆———————————

Who's Who Anyway?

If you decide you'd like to get some professional advice, it would probably be nice to have some idea where to begin.

John Smith (JS): Hello, Harold.

Harold Evensky (HE): Hi, and who am I speaking with?

JS: I'm John Smith, a reporter with the *Florida Times Journal Gazette*. I need a sentence or two on who provides investment advice to consumers.

HE: A sentence or two? This is a pretty big topic. It's often confusing even to us professionals.

JS: Maybe you can give me the gist of it.

HE: Well, I guess we could start with professionals known as money managers. They're the people who know all about picking stocks and bonds. They may not know what kinds of stocks or bonds you should be buying or even if you should be invested in stocks or bonds at all, but if you need to make those investments, money managers are the experts to hire.

JS: Okay. Where would you go to find these people?

HE: For most investors, the best place to find an experienced money manager is a mutual fund.

JS: A what?

HE: If you're a financial reporter, you must have heard of them. They're portfolios of stocks or bonds or international stocks or sometimes other assets, sometimes in combination, managed by some of the world's best money managers. They might not know a thing about you, the actual investor, but the better ones sure know about their portfolio.

JS: Okay, so I hire one of those—

HE: You don't want just one. You need to diversify sectors and styles. The good news is you can hire lots of these managers, each one a specialist in a different area of the economy: one for big U.S. companies, another to pick stocks in small U.S. companies, a third to find you the best foreign stocks, and then others who specialize in government bonds, or municipal bonds, or different flavors of corporate bonds. When you check out those managers, keep an eye out for a CFA designation. That stands for Chartered Financial Analyst and is an internationally respected credential for money managers.

JS: I see. Okay. I want to thank you—

HE: Wait. That's only one of many types of professionals you may need.

JS: What else could I want?

HE: Knowing how to pick stocks and bonds is terrific, but for individuals the most important question is how you decide how much to invest in stocks versus bonds.

JS: The money manager won't help me with that?

HE: That's the job of the expert known as the financial planner. That's a professional who is educated and experienced in helping individuals—such as your readers—make good financial decisions.

JS: Let me write this down. This is good stuff. So how does this financial planner decide if I should be in whatever those international or small things were?

HE: Financial planners follow a six-step process to help advice their clients. A credentialing body called the CFP Board of Standards—which I chaired some years back—defines this process. Basically it means that the financial planner gathers your personal and financial data, helps you define your goals, and analyzes where you are today financially. Only then will this person make recommendations and give you alternatives. When do you want to retire? What kind of lifestyle do you want to be able to afford when you do?

JS: And then I hire the money manager?

HE: Again, it's not manager but managers, and, yes, you could hire them on your own. However, with thousands of choices, most investors are better served letting a professional do the hiring for them. The financial planner will usually recommend a portfolio that will include several money managers in which he or she has confidence, in various investment sectors. Then the planner will monitor your progress toward your goals and watch over the money managers to make sure they're doing the best possible job for you.

JS: I'm not totally sure I understand the difference.

HE: The money manager is an expert on portfolios, but doesn't know a thing about *you*. For example, are you in a low or high tax bracket?

JS: I think I'm in a low one.

HE: Do you already have other investments that might overlap with the money manager's stocks? Do you need current cash flow from the investments? Are you comfortable with market volatility?

JS: Even *I* don't know the answer to these questions.

HE: The financial planner helps you understand and answer these questions. I could go on and on, but you get the point. It's the financial planner—the expert on people's financial needs—who will know all of that and much more about you.

JS: Do these financial planners also get the CFA designation?

HE: No, that's the professional designation for a money manager. In my opinion, the certified financial planner (CFP®) credential represents financial planning's highest standard. A professional holding the CFP mark has demonstrated not only knowledge of investments and planning but also an ability to apply that knowledge for your benefit.

JS: Does that mean that you're a CFP planner?

HE: Yes. But in fairness, there are two other respected credentials in the profession: the insurance industry's ChFC (chartered financial consultant) and the accounting profession's PFS (personal financial specialist).

JS: I think I have more than my two sentences. If there's anything else—

HE: There's a *lot* else.

JS: *[Sigh.]*

HE: Tell me about it. It's amazingly confusing for the poor consumer. Other types of designations reflect statutory registration or licensing requirements.

JS: Licensing? You mean like a licensed hair stylist?

HE: Some of these are actually sales licenses. Examples are the Series 7 licenses, which are required for advisors who earn commissions for selling investments, and the RIA (Registered Investment Advisor), a registration required of individuals who charge fees for providing investment advice. Depending on the business model used, a professional might be registered as an investment advisor as well as holding a securities license.

JS: I hope we're finished. Please tell me we're finished.

HE: Well, we haven't actually talked about what kind of professional I happen to be.

JS: *Sigh.* Which is?

HE: A wealth manager. The term *wealth manager,* as we use it, was introduced in a book, by that same name that I wrote for other professionals in the late 1990s. I defined it as a financial planning professional whose business specializes in a client's needs regarding investment and retirement planning.

JS: So that means you are—

HE: I'm a CFP licensee, and my firm is a financial planning firm specializing in what we call *wealth management.*

JS: I don't think any sane person could keep track of all this.

HE: If you have to remember only one thing, then understand that current laws do not ensure that all professionals providing investment advice are looking out for your best interests.

JS: Don't I want somebody serving my best interests? I don't want to pay somebody to convince me to buy something that earns more for their company than it does for me.

HE: Now you're getting it.

JS: So what do I do?

HE: If you want my best advice, no matter who you ultimately select to guide you, your best protection is to ask the advisor to sign a simple, "mom-and-pop" commitment acknowledging that they're really looking out for your best interest.

JS: Can you send me a copy?

HE: I will. Be sure and use it for your own protection.

And I did. Below is the document I sent.

I believe in placing your best interests first. Therefore, I am proud to commit to the following five principles:

- I will always put your best interests first.

- I will act with prudence—with the skill, care, diligence, and good judgment of a professional.

- I will not mislead you, and I will provide conspicuous, full, and fair disclosure of all important facts.

- I will avoid conflicts of interest.

- I will fully disclose and fairly manage, in your favor, any unavoidable conflicts.

Advisor_____

CHAPTER 10

REAL CASH FLOW:

———————◆———————

A Fix for the Fixed Income

Charlie Jacobs (CJ): Hello, Harold. May I call you Harold?

Harold Evensky: I guess it depends. Who are you and how did you end up in my office?

CJ: My name is Charlie Jacobs. I'm a wholesaler for the Special Income Portfolio.

HE: Charlie, I have to ask you this: how did you get past the receptionist? I don't normally take cold meetings with mutual fund wholesalers or fund salespeople. I prefer to speak to them after I've done my own preliminary analysis.

CJ: Actually, I waited until your receptionist was distracted by another guest, and then I crawled along the floor until I reached the hallway and slipped past the doors of your other coworkers as soon as they turned their heads away from the door.

HE: That's quite remarkable. All right, Ninja wholesaler, now that you're here, have a seat. What can I do for you?

CJ: I'm here to convince you to recommend the Special Income Portfolio to all of your clients. I even brought some golf balls as a nice gift to get the conversation started.

HE: You can keep the golf balls. Just tell me the facts about your fund. This could turn into a very quick visit.

CJ: It's an income fund. Some of your clients are retired, aren't they?

HE: Yes, they are.

CJ: And they need income from their investments to supplement their pension and Social Security to support their lifestyle. By the way, if you don't play golf, I brought candy. Or maybe you're interested in one of these cute little jump drives with our company's logo on it.

HE: My retired clients need cash flow from their investments to supplement their other income sources, and I don't want or need candy or one of those jump drives.

CJ: Well, the Special Income Portfolio is carefully designed to give your clients exactly what they need in the form of dividends and interest. It's invested in companies that pay high dividends and bonds that pay high income. I have a little form you can fill out so you can start moving your clients' assets over right away—

HE: Hold on a minute. You just hit one of my hot buttons. Maybe you should sit back and relax. This could take longer than either of us expected.

CJ: What do you mean?

HE: I have to confess that I've got a lot of pet peeves about the kind of nonsense that gets foisted on the public as good investment advice. But one of my biggest is what I call *the myth of dividends and interest.*

CJ: I can assure you that our portfolio manager doesn't invest in myths.

HE: What you're saying probably sounds plausible to 99 percent of the investing public. Of course, many investors need cash flow from their portfolio. So you put the words *income fund* in the name of a mutual fund, and it sounds exactly like what people need.

CJ: It *is* what people need.

HE: I disagree. We plan for a lot more than a *fixed income.* We plan for a consistent *real income.*

CJ: I'm not sure I follow you.

HE: I'll make it easy. Does the carton of milk you bought last week, your last doctor's visit, or your last new car cost more than it did five, ten, or fifteen years ago?

CJ: Of course.

HE: And do you think all those things and everything else will cost more in the next twenty to thirty years?

CJ: Probably lots more.

HE: Today's dollar isn't what it used to be and tomorrow it won't be worth what it is today. Do you agree? Don't you think you and I and everyone else will need more of those greenbacks in the future just to hold our own?

CJ: Yes, I suppose we will.

HE: How long have you been doing this work as a wholesaler?

CJ: Oh, I have weeks of experience. I know my way around, let me assure you.

HE: Somewhere in your sales training, you heard that professionals use the term *real* dollars to mean an amount of money that will buy the same goods and services (milk, doctor's visits, and cars) in the future as it will today. A *real* dollar means the same purchasing power going forward.

CJ: I think I have that somewhere in my notes, yes. But I think you're missing the point. When someone retires, he or she needs a fixed income.

HE: What horsepucky!

CJ: Excuse me?

HE: Dangerous advice like that really infuriates me. If people plan a retirement based on a fixed income, they had better be planning on changing their diet from steaks to cat food throughout the balance of their lifetime. What retirees need is an income that will increase every year by the inflation rate. Other than winning the lottery, that's the only way people can maintain their standard of living.

CJ: We also have a lottery fund that invests in a diversified portfolio of state lottery tickets that I could show you—

HE: Let's go back to deciding what kind of investments my clients need to make in order to supplement their pension and Social Security income. Suppose they buy into this *myth* you're selling and construct an "income" portfolio.

CJ: Great idea! That's exactly the fund I want to talk to you about.

HE: Now they have a portfolio bond/stock allocation that is largely fixed by design—inappropriate design. In almost all cases, it will cause an inferior portfolio for two reasons: Not only will the portfolio not allow them to accomplish their goals in real dollars, but it will also be inefficient.

CJ: Okay, I understand that you have objections.

HE: What do you mean?

CJ: The sales training said that I should overcome your objections, and the first step is to get your objections out in the open. So tell me your objections.

HE: With pleasure. In fact, I'll draw you a picture. Here's an example I use when discussing this issue with my clients. Consider a simple world in which you have only three investment choices—a money market, Bond Fund A, and Stock Fund B. In this world, the investments will provide exactly the returns I'm writing down in this simple table:

Investment	Interest	Dividends	Capital Gains	Total Return
Bond Fund A	7%	0%	0%	7%
Stock Fund B	0%	3%	10%	13%

Does that look right?

CJ: It could be.

HE: Now suppose you've saved $200,000 for retirement and you need $14,000 a year from your savings to add to your Social Security and pension income. If you planned to get your needed $14,000 cash flow from dividends and interest, you would have to invest 100 percent in the Bond Fund. The reason is because, as you can see from this table I'm now drawing, the cash flow from Stock Fund B's dividend payments is so low, any amount invested in stocks would drop your cash flow to an amount less than the $14,000 you need.

BOND A CASH FLOW STOCK B CASH FLOW

Allocation from Bond	Allocation from Stock	Total Cash Flow
90 percent $12,600	10 percent $ 600	$13,200
50 percent $7,000	50 percent $3,000	$10,000
40 percent $5,600	60 percent $3,600	$9,200

CJ: Doesn't that make my point?

HE: No. Because if you look at the future, then the purchasing power of that $14,000 starts to decline. Let's say you're retired, and I recommend the all Bond Fund. You might feel good today receiving the $14,000 you need; however, how would you feel ten years later if inflation had been 3 percent and your $14,000 only bought $10,417 worth of stuff?

CJ: I'd be calling my attorney to see if I had grounds for a lawsuit against you.

HE: And what happens twenty years later, when your diet has switched from steak to cat food, because that's all you can afford?

CJ: I don't like where this is going.

HE: I don't want to give my clients fixed income when they need real income from a long-term portfolio that has an allocation to investments that are likely to rise in value and provide protection against inflation. In other words, I don't want to guarantee that my clients will suffer losses in real-dollar terms. And that's what you're offering me.

CJ: Is that your objection?

HE: My objection is that investors do not need dividends or interest—they need real cash flow. So they shouldn't fall for this myth that you're selling about dividends and interest. Now you can feel free to overcome my objections, if you want. And please put those golf balls away.

CJ: Actually, I was wondering if I should move *my* money out of the fund.

HE: If you're planning to live more than a couple of years, you might think about it.

CJ: Thanks, Harold. Thanks for the advice. Are you sure you don't want one of these jump drives?

CHAPTER 11

TAXES:

———————◆———————

It Pays to Treat Them Right

I know how most people feel about taxes: don't tax me, don't tax thee, tax the man behind the tree. Unfortunately, ultimately we gotta pay. Everyone's interested in minimizing the pain and that's why I'm sitting here trying to put together a talk on tax planning for our local Rotary Club. It's a great group of sophisticated professionals, and I don't want to talk down to them, but I do want to provide some useful information.

Trying to balance those issues reminded me of a complaint one of my client's accountant had about how we had selected some of his bond investments. I remembered that sophisticated doesn't necessarily mean knowledgeable. So here's what I came up with:

DON'T LET THE TAX TAIL WAG THE DOG

The accountant's complaint about our choice of bonds was a result of his focusing on the tax tail. Our client was in a moderately high tax bracket; however, we had his short-term, fixed-income investments in corporate bonds. "Move 'em to tax-free municipals" was the accountant's advice. Well, it's true, our clients would have paid less tax if we'd invested them in municipal bonds, but they would also have had a lower after-tax return. Why? At the time, taxable bonds were paying 5 percent and similar quality and maturity municipals were paying 3¼ percent. That meant our 30 percent marginal tax bracket client had a choice of earning 3¼ percent with no tax obligation or 5 percent with the obligation of paying 30 percent of his interest payments to Uncle Sam. Which would you choose? I hope the 5 percent.

Even if you peel off the 30 percent tax bite, that would leave 3½ percent in your pocket. It's not rocket science to see that 3½ percent is better than 3¼ percent. The moral? When choosing between equivalent-quality taxable and tax-free investments, don't worry about how much you'll have to pay Uncle Sam (even if painful). Instead, keep your eye focused on how much you'll have after paying taxes.

TURNOVER DOESN'T TELL ALL

It's common for investors to use turnover as a measure of tax efficiency. Don't do it. When you look at an investment's turnover number, it's natural to think it represents a pro-rata turnover of all the securities in the portfolio. For example, a 60 percent turnover would mean that 60 percent of the positions in the portfolio are sold in one year. Sound reasonable? As my brother, the economist, would say, *au contraire.* A 60 percent turnover doesn't necessarily mean that 60 percent of the stocks have been traded. It might well mean 20 percent of the stocks have been traded three times. All of those trades may have been the sale of stocks with losses, not gains, so the manager not only generated no tax bite, he also realized losses that can shelter future gains.

AND THE REST OF THE STORY (THE MOST IMPORTANT PART)

Taxes are a function of something called a *holding period*, not turnover. The holding period is the average number of years it would require to turn over all of the positions in the portfolio. To explain: let's assume that the manager has a portfolio chock full of stocks with taxable gains and he is trading all of the stock in his portfolio pro rata. So a 20 percent portfolio turnover would mean one-fifth of the stocks would be sold each year, or 100 percent in five years. That means, on average, the manager holds stocks for two and a half years.

Obviously, a portfolio with a 90 percent turnover would realize pretty much all of the gains in the first year, which means lots of taxes; consequently, a 50 percent turnover sounds a *lot* better. But if you think about it, 50 percent means selling one-half this year and paying the taxes, and one-half next year with more taxes. The difference between paying all of the taxes in year one versus one-half of them in year one and one-half in year two is negligible. The graph below shows the relationship. Unless turnover is *very* low—less than 10–15 percent, there is no real tax efficiency.

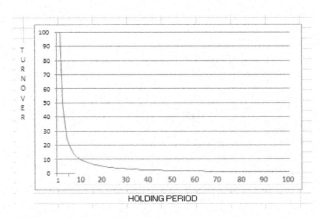

The moral? Avoid the murky middle. A few years ago, my partner, Deena Katz, and I co-edited a book called the *Investment Think Tank* (Bloomberg Press). We invited several friends (practitioners and academics) to contribute chapters on subjects they believed were of vital importance for advisors.

Recognizing the importance of the holding period, Jean Brunel, managing principal of Brunel Associates, introduced the concept of the murky middle. He noted that the more active the manager, the more you'd expect him to add value. After all, why would you want to pay the trading cost and suffer the tax inefficiency of active trading if you weren't rewarded with extra net returns? He also noted the reality of the elbow graph above: no matter the manager's intention, as turnover increases a tax-efficient manager will be no more tax efficient than a tax-oblivious manager.

Brunel's excellent advice is to avoid the murky middle—hire very low-turnover managers (indexes and ETFs) when you want to just capture market returns. Hire go-go, active managers with the funds you're prepared to invest at higher risk to earn better-than-market returns. Stay away from those managers who, for marketing purposes, try to straddle the fence, going for both tax efficiency and extra return. They may have performance numbers that look good before taxes, but after taxes, the numbers don't look so good. Here's how Brunel depicts the murky middle:

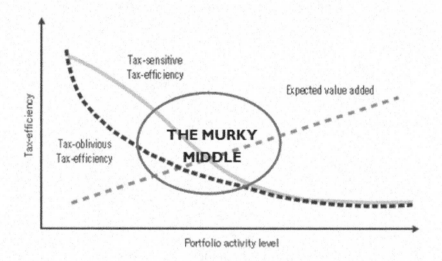

I think my Rotary audience will like this talk. For more on the murky middle, check out Chapter 3, "Net, Net, Net: Expenses, Taxes, and Inflation Can Eat Your Nest Egg – What To Do?"

CHAPTER 12

PASCAL'S WAGER:

———◆———

The 0.1 Percent Risk

Playing Russian roulette with a thousand-chamber gun might not seem so risky, until you consider the consequence of that 0.1 percent risk.

I've been working with Linda, my client, for the last hour entering data into MoneyGuide, our planning program. We're now discussing the plan's time horizon—how long her nest egg needs to last so she can keep groceries on the table.

"Linda," I asked her, "one of the major guesses we need to make is how long you will need money." (That's my tactful way of asking what age she thinks she'll die.)

Years ago, we used a standard actuarial table to estimate how long someone might live. Unfortunately, as a thoughtful friend pointed out, that means you'd have a 50 percent chance of outliving your nest egg, so today we use an age that, based on your current health, your family's health history, and if you are or are not a smoker, represents a 30 percent chance of your reaching that age. (Chapter 15, Life Timing. What Lynn Hopewell Teach Us?")

"Linda," I continued, "based on your current health and your family health history, we should consider using age ninety-three for planning."

"Harold, you must be kidding. I'll never make it to ninety-three! Let's use eighty-five."

"Sounds like a nice number. How did you decide on eighty-five?"

"Well, actually no particular calculation. It just seems like a reasonable age to use and I want to be reasonable in my planning."

"Tell me, Linda, are you familiar with Pascal's wager?"

"Pascal's what?"

"Pascal's wager is a philosophical construct devised by the seventeenth-century mathematician, Blaise Pascal. Here's my version: If you knew for certain there was only a 10 percent chance that God exists, you would have two ways to live your life: You could conclude the probability of God's existence was so low you'd elect to ignore morals and ethics and live a totally outrageous life. If, when you died, it turned out that there really is no God, hence no consequences for your immoral life, you lucked out. Of course, if, when you died, you discovered God was not a myth and you found yourself chest high in fire and brimstone, where you'd be roasting for eternity, you might not be very pleased with your choice.

"On the other hand, suppose you decided that, even with the low odds, you would live a moral and ethical life. If, when you died, you discovered there is no God, you would still have lived a comfortable life. If there is a God and you're rewarded in heaven for your exemplary life, you will have won the eternal lottery."

"So, what's this got to do with retirement planning?"

The answer is *everything*! All too often in planning, we get caught up with the power of probability. Live until ninety-three? Possible, but not likely, so I want to make plans based on living until age eighty-five. Based on probabilities, that's not an unreasonable response. However, as Pascal taught us, that conclusion is missing an important half of the equation, namely, the consequences. Often the terrible negative consequence of coming out on the short side of the probability overwhelms the low probability.

Let's suppose Linda does live only until age eighty-five. That means she can spend more between now and then because her money doesn't have to last for another seven years. Good outcome.

Suppose she lives well beyond eighty-five. If we use eighty-five, as a planning age, that means by eighty-six, if her plan works out as expected, her nest egg will be approaching $0! The consequences of living another seven years supported solely by her Social Security income? That means reducing her standard of living by about two-thirds, which may not be on a par with fire and brimstone forever but it's high on the quality-of-life disaster scale. The moral? Don't just consider probabilities when planning—consider the consequences.vfgrcg

"Still want to plan only to eighty-five, Linda?"

CHAPTER 13

THE THREE PS OF
INVESTING:

Philosophy, Process and People

In Real Estate, it's location, location, location. In investing, it's philosophy, process, and people. Most investors look at past performance when evaluating a manager. That's a rearview mirror approach. If you're driving forward, keeping your eyes on the rearview mirror is dangerous. Looking backward is equally dangerous for investors. You can't buy past performance, so don't invest based just on looking backward. To avoid that mistake, here's a simple process that works for any investment manager you might hire—mutual funds, separate accounts, or alternatives.

PHILOSOPHY

When you are evaluating money managers, find out what their investment philosophy is. What is their unique view of the investment world? How is it different from those of their competitors? Is it credible that a manager can overcome the drag of expenses and taxes and provide risk-adjusted returns better than other alternatives? Basically, you're looking for a good and credible story. How might you find it? Read the manager's letters, prospectus and marketing material; look for something more than "we buy low and sell high."

PROCESS

A good story is nice, but how does the manager make it work in the real world? Answers to this question may be harder to pin down, but remember, it's your hard-earned money at risk.

PEOPLE

Philosophy and process are essential, but ultimately it's people who make the difference. People will be making investment decisions about your money.

Don Phillips is a managing director and board member of Morningstar. He is a good friend of mine and one of the most-respected professionals in finance. He has some simple advice regarding people: "You want people with passion for the job of money manager."

Did the managers you are considering invent the firm's philosophy and process or have they at least been around long enough to have developed a passion for it? If not, even if the investment passes the test of the first two Ps, move on to your next investment alternative.

TESTING THE PS

In this conversation with a gentleman I will call Happy Promoter, I put the three Ps to the test.

Happy Promoter (HP): Good morning, Mr. Evensky. My name is Happy Promoter. I'm familiar with your firm and I appreciate your taking the time to see me this morning.

Harold Evensky (HE): Mr. Promoter, it's my pleasure. I understand you represent Sophisticated Hedge Fund Strategies and you have a new offering available. My friend Mr. Jones suggested I meet with you; I'm always interested in learning about new potential investments for our clients. Please tell me about your program.

HP: It's a very sophisticated long-short strategy based on an evaluation of a myriad of market dynamics that guide our trading algorithms to ensure that we provide consistent alpha in all markets. Because we can profit in both rising and falling markets, we can mitigate downside risk, and by the judicious use of margin, we can provide returns that significantly exceed the S&P 500. We've backtested our strategy for the last ten years and the results substantiate the success of our strategy.

Well, at this point, I'm thinking I need to know a lot more before I take Mr. Promoter's pitch seriously. Backtesting is a common but questionable way of evaluating a new investment strategy. It mathematically simulates how the strategy would have fared if it had existed in the past. One obvious problem is that unless the strategy is 100 percent automatic—no active decisions or modifications are made by the manager along the way—there is no way of knowing if the simulation is a fair representation of how the strategy will be implemented in the future. An even bigger problem is that there's no reason to believe that future markets will mirror the historical environment used for the backtesting. Bottom line: because it theoretically would have worked in the past is no reason to believe it will succeed in the future. The financial world is full of failed investment strategies that had wonderful backtest results.

So, I decide I need to take Mr. Promoter through the process I call the "three Ps."

HE: Mr. Promoter, what you've said sounds good, but I need more meat to the story. Can you tell me what your basic investment philosophy is? What do you see in the financial markets that the thousands of other professional investment managers don't? After all, the market is a zero-sum game. For everyone who makes a buck, there has to be someone else losing one.

HP: Harold—may I call you Harold?

HE: Certainly.

HP: We believe that our sophisticated algorithms will provide the edge.

HE: I understand that, but can you be more specific?

HP: No, I'm afraid that our process is quite confidential and proprietary.

HE: Well then, can you at least give me some details about the procedures you use to implement your sophisticated process?

HP: Good lord, no! Our system is a black box and all the details are carefully guarded secrets. It's the "secret sauce" that enables us to provide the low-volatility, high returns your clients are seeking.

HE: I see. Then I guess I'd have to look to the experience and quality of the intellectual capital behind your strategy. Will you tell me who developed your sophisticated strategy and what experience they have in implementing it?

HP: Harold, I'm the lead creator of the strategy and I'm supported by a two-man team of MBAs. My educational background is a master's in History; however, I've been fascinated by the market for decades and I spent the last few years studying market movements. I finished developing my strategy just last month. I know that as a sophisticated practitioner you're aware that alternative managers with well-established track records work only with large institutional clients and have no interest in dealing in the retail market, so a new manager such as I can provide your clients with the best alternative.

Mr. Promoter seemed like a nice guy, but he miserably failed the three Ps, so I thanked him for his time. My only thought after this brief meeting was, *"What a waste of time; wait until I get hold of Jones!"*

CHAPTER 14

MARKET TIMING FOR FUN AND SOMEONE ELSE'S PROFIT:

Don't Do It

A broker stands looking out of the window of his sumptuous office down at the marina thirty stories below with his client at his side. "See those yachts down there?" says the broker to his client. "The one on the left is mine, the one in the middle is my partner's, and the one on the right is our office manager's."

"Where are your clients' yachts?"

David Samuel: Hello, Harold. It's David Samuel again. I know you have that AAII meeting coming up next week, but this can't wait. My brother said he just got a call from his broker, who told him to bail out of the market at least for the next few months because the firm's technicians said they see a major correction coming within weeks. I assume you've probably seen the same and agree, but I just wanted to double-check.

Harold Evensky: David, I just want to be sure I have this straight. You're saying the broker is confident enough in his crystal ball to say that everyone should run to cash?

DS: You got it.

HE: Hum, I know he works for a big wire house; I wonder if that firm has moved all its money to cash? I don't think so, because a move of that magnitude would have made the papers, and none of the managers we monitor have made significant liquidations recently. It somewhat makes you wonder what your brother's broker knows that no one else does.

DS: Well, I understand that he's been in the business for decades and he's a senior VP at the firm, so he must know something.

HE: I'm sure he knows how to sell, because the impressive title comes with generating big commissions for the firm. There are many quality SVPs who earn their commissions from long-term quality advice.

Unfortunately, there are some who succeed by focusing on generating commissions independent of the client's needs. That's the basis for the old joke: "How do you make $1,000,000 in the market? Start with $2,000,000." In deciding whether market-timing advice is something you want to follow, remember, when market timing, a broker earns a commission for the sale of each and every one of the positions their clients sell *and* another commission when they repurchase those positions. Here are a few things you might want to consider:

Can you name the top ten musicians of all time? The top ten baseball players? The top ten presidents? Of course, you can. We might argue about the list but most people can make up a list.

Now, tell me the top ten market timers of all time? Can't even name one, can you? Your brother's broker may be the first, but do you really want to bet on that?

What do market reality and statistics tell us? There are innumerable problems with market timing, including transaction and tax drag. But there are two major problems. You have to make *two* correct calls: 1) when to get out *and* 2) when to get back in. Factoring in transactions and taxes, research indicates you need to be correct about 70 percent of the time.

Markets don't just drop precipitously, but they recover quickly, so waiting for confirmation of the end of a bear market usually means missing a significant part of the recovery. That makes for a tough hurdle.

For example: In a study covering the period 1987–2007, research found that the annualized return for someone invested for 5,296 days was 11.5 percent. Unfortunately, if you missed the ten best days (less than 2/10 of 1 percent), your return would have dropped to 8 percent,

Why would you be likely to miss those best days? Because those best days occurred within two weeks of a worst day 70 percent of the time. And they occurred within six months of a best day 100 percent of the time!

In an industry study in 2008, researchers found that although the annualized market return for the prior twenty years was 11.6 percent, the average stock fund investor earned a paltry 4.5 percent. It turned out that for most investors, market timing was mighty expensive. And, David, unless you've recently obtained a working crystal ball, it's likely to also prove costly for you.

To make money in the market, you have to be in the market through thick and thin. In fact, if you remember our discussion on rebalancing, you'll remember that bear markets are great buying opportunities for long-term investors. So, my advice is to stop listening to so-called experts spouting nonsense and go back to making money in your business.

CHAPTER 15

LIFE TIMING:

———◆———

What Did Lynn Hopewell Teach Us?

You're not average, so don't plan the quality of the rest of your life based on averages.

I was sitting front row center in a big conference room at our national planning symposium; I'd been looking forward to this talk for a while. The speaker, financial planner Lynn Hopewell, was a good friend and one of the most thoughtful practitioners I knew. My partner, Deena, and I had been responsible for planning this program and we invited Hopewell to speak because he told us he had a few major concepts he wanted to share with his peers. Here's what he shared that day:

AND END NOT SO NEAR

Welcome, everyone. I have few stories to tell that I hope will be a wake-up call for the financial planning profession. The first is about my planning for an engineering client, Ms. Jane. She is sixty-three, a very successful and accomplished civil engineer, and president of a major structural engineering firm. She hired me to work with her in developing a comprehensive retirement plan. Well, since I too am an old engineer, I know how they think—detail, detail! So I worked very hard to provide Ms. Jane a plan that would resonate with her. Finally, I was sitting down with her, ready to blow her socks off, and after going through my complete analysis, I thought I had.

"Mr. Hopewell," she said, "I'm very impressed with the thoroughness and depth of your plan. I have only one small question."

Well, needless to say, I was beaming at the compliment and looked forward to answering her "one small question."

She went on, "I understand that selecting a mortality age—the age the plan assumes I die and will no longer need income—is a critical element in the planning process.

"Obviously," I said, "if we arbitrarily use a very old age, such as one hundred, we're likely to have to tell you to reduce your spending so that your nest egg will last to that age. Of course, if you die before one hundred, you'll be leaving a lot of money on the table that you could have enjoyed spending while you were alive. If we assume a much younger age and you're long-lived, the consequences could be even worse because you'd run out of money before you ran out of time. As a consequence, we work hard to select a reasonable planning age."

"That makes sense to me," she said, "and I understand that the age you selected for the plan is based on the projected age of my death from a national mortality table."

"Correct! And not just any mortality table. We spent quite a bit of time consulting with actuaries to determine which table reflected the most current actuarial data."

"I understood that. What I'm still a little confused about is the meaning of that age. As I understand it, if the table says my mortality age is eighty-eight, that means half the people will have died by eighty-eight and half will still be alive."

"Correct."

"Well, doesn't that mean if I plan to age eighty-eight, I'll have a 50 percent chance of outliving my plan?"

That question hit me like a Mack truck. Ms. Jane was correct. Even worse, in thinking about it, I realized that anyone with the resources to need the advice of a financial planner was likely to have had better health care and nutrition than the average of the universe of individuals making up the mortality table. That means Ms. Jane had better than a 50 percent chance of outliving my plan. This was a major wake-up call for me and should be for any practitioner relying on a traditional mortality table. Lynn said, "After acknowledging Ms. Jane's point and scheduling a follow-up visit to give me time to consider the ramifications of her simple question, I hunkered down in my office to consider how I might resolve this problem."

So, I went back to my own office and did the same. After additional conversations with my actuary friends, I concluded that a reasonable solution would be to use more customized actuarial tables—those that allowed me to factor in whether the client is a smoker, nonsmoker, her current health, and whether the lifespan of her immediate family is long, average, or short. Then, using the appropriate customized table, we would select an age that represented only a 30 percent chance of her outliving the age indicated in the table.

Here's an example that shows how big a range the mortality age can be depending on these factors:

	Nonsmoker			Smoker		
Avg Health:	Excellent	Excellent	Average	Average	Poor	Excellent
Avg Family:	Long Lives	Short	Poor	Average	Short	Poor
Plan Age	93	88	87	85	81	85

Obviously, there is no guarantee that the age selected will coincide with the client's mortality; however, following this process is likely to provide a much more realistic estimate.

Well, Lynn was right. That was a major wake-up call, because I'd been using a standard actuarial table and mortality age for my planning assumption. That was about to change.

Even if Lynn had stopped there, this information would have justified all of the time and cost of attending the three-day symposium, but there was more. Lynn's next story was about the ah-ha moment he had one day when developing a college funding recommendation.

COLLEGE CALCULATIONS

Not long ago I was preparing a simple college funding recommendation for a client. You know how that goes. It's a simple time-value calculation that requires input on how many years until college, how many years of college the client wants to pay for, the annual cost, and the college tuition inflation rate. My input looks something like this:

> Years to college - 4   Years in college - 4   Annual cost - $40,000
> College costs inflation - 6%   Investment return - 8%

A financial calculation would result in a recommendation that the client set aside about $145,000 to fund this expense. When I presented this to the client, he asked how confident I was about my number. When I thought about his question, I realized the answer was not very. My estimate was what we refer to as a "point estimate." This means that unless every assumption I made was exactly right, my recommendation would either over- or underfund the college tuition bill.

As a former engineer, I remembered that when trying to estimate the probability of uncertain events, we used a technique known as a "Monte Carlo simulation." Developed at Los Alamos National Laboratory during the Second World War for the design of nuclear weapons, Monte Carlo is really a simple concept. Rather than making a single guess regarding a possible outcome, we make guesses about the likely ranges of the outcomes.

We then simulate thousands of possible futures with different combinations of those possible outcomes.

Let's expand the table I showed a minute ago to more realistically reflect the uncertainty in our estimates.

What we know with some certainty:

- Years to college 4

- What we're making an educated guess about

- Tuition somewhere between

- Annual cost $30,000 to $50,000

- College costs inflation 5 to 7 percent

- Investment return 6 to 10 percent

With these ranges, there are many thousands of possible outcomes, for example:

	Scenario #1	Scenario #2	Scenario #3	Scenario #4
Annual cost	$32,500	$47,200	$43,100	$36,400
College costs inflation	5.1%	6.2%	5.7%	6.4%
Investment return	7.9%	9.1%	6.4%	8.6%

The Monte Carlo simulation calculates for each of these examples how much money that investors would need to set aside today if they want to fully fund four years of education. If the analysis ran a thousand examples, the results, listed in order of decreasing savings, might look something like this:

Simulation	Answer
1	$134,000
2	$137,000
3	$142,000
4	$143,000
5	$144,000
799	$165,000
800	$167,000
801	$169,000
998	$182,000
999	$184,000
1000	$189,000

In this case, the question was how much should you put away now if you want an 80 percent probability of meeting your goal? The answer would be $167,000, because 80 percent (800/1,000) of the simulations would have succeeded with that amount of savings or less.

Well, this was another major wake-up call for me. In hindsight, it seemed obvious that a point estimate was inappropriate and that a Monte Carlo simulation could provide a more meaningful answer. In wrapping up his discussion, Lynn reminded us that expanding the input matrix meant making more guesses. Despite the mathematical rigor of a Monte Carlo simulation, adding more guesses does not justify adding two more decimal places to the answer. His point was that we should use Monte Carlo as an educational tool and not suggest it is a mathematically accurate answer.

THE TAKEAWAYS

When planning retirement, don't assume average mortality—you're not average.

When attempting to quantify an uncertain future, don't default to a single estimate. Use a Monte Carlo simulation to develop an understanding of the likelihood of possible outcomes, but don't take the results as gospel.

PART 3:

ALL ABOUT YOU

CHAPTER 16

ASSET ALLOCATION:

———◆━━◆━━━

The Myth of the Portfolio that Acts your Age

Policy research is great for policy makers but may be poison for you.

I just finished reading an article in a professional journal that reported on extensive research about how people of different ages divide their investments between stocks and bonds. It went something like this.

Our research, based on zillions of responses to trillions of questions, has determined that investors at age forty have 60 percent of their funds in stocks and 40 percent in bonds. Investors at age seventy have 70 percent in bonds and 30 percent in stock. Further analysis, to a high degree of statistical significance, has determined these proportions are close to the proper allocation of resources for the average investor of these age groups.

Therefore, we have concluded that, based on our studies, investors should use the following formula to determine the percentage of stocks and bonds in their portfolios:

- The amount to be invested in stocks = (100 – the investor's age)

- The amount to be invested in bonds = (100 – the amount invested in stock)

What a terrific solution to how you should invest your money. No muss, no fuss. All you need to know is your age and the rest is just simple math that you can do in your head. If that seems too easy, there are many companies and magazines that provide more detailed suggestions about how to invest your money based on your age. All of these approaches are based on a concept known as life-cycle investing. The general idea is that your financial needs are related to your age. The approach is endlessly popular and sounds terrific. There's only one problem: it's hogwash!

Wait, that's not fair. If you happen to be a sociologist or a government policy maker, this might be terrific stuff. After all, sociology is the study of large groups. Still, it's dangerous hogwash if you try to use it to plan your own life. Remember, sociologists are the professionals who came up with the concept of families with 1.8 parents and 2.3 children.

Since you're probably not a sociologist or policy maker, and are more interested in your unique needs than the statistically average needs of everyone your current age, the cookie cutter—life cycle approach—to planning won't work for you.

Let me tell you about two of my clients, the Salters and the Boones. When we first worked with them, my partners and I were amazed at how similar these two families seemed. Both families not only live in the same city, they also live in the same neighborhood, just two blocks apart, in houses of the same model, built the same year by the same builder. Mr. and Mrs. Salter and Mr. and Mrs. Boone are working professionals. When we met them they each were fifty-five years old, in good health, and they planned on retiring when they reached sixty-two. The coincidences seemed endless. We thought they even *looked* alike! Both had investment portfolios valued at $1,000,000 at that point, and they all considered themselves moderately conservative investors. Because neither the Salters nor Boones have children, they have no desire to leave an estate.

Well, if lifestyle planning worked, these two couples' investment portfolios should look alike. Lucky for our clients we are financial planners and we gathered more information. Here's what we discovered:

Client Wealth and Retirement Goals

	Current Investments Total	Annual Preretirement Savings (Per Year)	After Tax Standard of Living	Social Security
Salters	$1,000,000	$20,000	$57,000	$22,000
Boones	$1,000,000	$0	$73,000	$12,000

How about that? To a sociologist, these couples looked alike; to a financial planner, based on their savings rate, their retirement income, and financial goals they looked very different. Let's see how our recommendations differed from the life-cycle solution.

Life-Cycle Recommendations

	Stock	Bonds
100 – Age	43%	57%

Note that the life-cycle recommendation is the same for the Salters and Boones. That seems a little strange because the Boones plan on spending a lot more than the Salters in retirement, and the Salters are saving more between now and retirement and have significantly more Social Security income. The fact that their ages, risk tolerance, employment, home, health, and planned retirement dates are similar is irrelevant.

After careful analysis and based on the information specific to our clients, we made the following recommendations:

Wealth Manager Recommendations

	Bonds	Stock
Salters	35%	60%
Boones	65%	40%

It sure doesn't look like the 55 percent bond formula you'd get by subtracting their age from one hundred. Why the difference? In spite of similar demographics, the Salters and Boones have very different resources and goals. Remember, you're unique and planning based on simple rules of thumb can be a mighty dangerous way to plan the quality of the rest of your life.

CHAPTER 17

IRRATIONAL INVESTING:

You're Not the only One Who's Nuts

Good news! You're not irrational, you're human.

I just came from one of the most exciting lectures I've ever attended. That shouldn't be a big surprise, because Danny Kahneman, the speaker, is a Nobel Laureate. Professor Kahneman received the Nobel Prize in economics for what has become known as Behavioral Economics. Basically, his studies brought to light the difference between the rational investor—someone who always rationally makes investment decisions in his or her best financial interest—and real people like you and me. We live in a complex world and that's certainly true of investing.

To manage the complexities of life, we often use something called *heuristics* to help us efficiently make decisions in spite of complexities. Think of heuristics as mental shortcuts. Most of the time, these shortcuts work out well; unfortunately, they sometimes result in our making decisions that, when looked at objectively, seem irrational. Each of us also comes complete with a bunch of cognitive biases that lead us to create our own reality, which may not be consistent with the real world. Let me share some examples from Professor Kahneman's lecture.

BUILT-IN BIAS

Just after being introduced, Kahneman asked everyone to look at the audience in the room (there were about one hundred financial planners in attendance). After a few seconds of our rubbernecking, he asked us to raise our hands if we believed that the quality of our planning advice is above the average represented by the other planners in the room. Well, surprise, surprise, we were all above average—just like Garrison Keeler's Lake Woebegone, where all of the kids are above average.

The problem, of course, is that's not rational. Half of the audience must have been below average. Professor Kahneman explained that as humans we have an innate overconfidence bias that leads us to have confidence in our judgment—a confidence greater than objective accuracy would suggest. How, he asked, might that get us into trouble when investing? Lots of ways.

We are often overconfident in our ability to pick investments or in the abilities of the money manager we love or the ability of financial media mavens to guide us to the best investments.

Kahneman told the audience about the research of Terry Odean and Brad Barber, University of California professors, who studied the trading results of almost seventy thousand households during a six-year period, accounting for about two million buys and sales. They found that investors who traded the most—those with the most confidence and the best ideas— earned an annual return 11.4 percent. The problem was that the market return was 17.9 percent. The professors' conclusion? Overconfidence in your good idea may be hazardous to your wealth.

The best protection we have against overconfidence is to step back and apply a strong dose of humility and skepticism before we act.

Next, Kahneman put up a slide that looked something like this:

HHTHTTHTTH

TTTTTTTTTT

He explained that it represented the results of tossing two coins ten times. He and asked which one we thought was the fair coin and which one was bogus. As sophisticated practitioners we knew instantly that the second coin was bogus: Ten tails in a row? Give me a break. In hindsight, I'm embarrassed to say we fell for the heuristic called *representativeness*. You know the one: if it walks like a duck and quacks like a duck, it must be a duck.

The problem is that the randomness heuristic led us astray. Had we stopped to think it through, we would have realized that getting ten tails in a row is just as random as the first toss series; the problem was it didn't *look* random. Our brains, knowing a coin toss is random, took a shortcut and concluded that toss one looked random so it was authentic; toss two was obviously not random, so it must be bogus.

How can that get us in investment trouble? Ever consider investing in a fund with a Morningstar rating of less than four or five stars? Probably not; bad mistake. Use the star information as one element in your selection process, but the Morningstar ratings are not guarantees of future superior performance. You need to do a lot more research than simply defaulting to the stars as the sole selection criterion. Doing so puts you at serious risk of picking a loser and rejecting a superior investment.

MUDDLED MATH

Professor Kahneman also introduced us to the work of Professor Dick Thaler on mental accounting. It seems that in addition to occasionally being misled by our heuristics and biases, we also stumble over what would seem to be simple math. I know this from personal experience with my clients. I remember having a visit after the tech bust from a retired surgeon, who came into my office almost in tears.

"Harold, I don't understand. Last year I made 80 percent on my investments and this year I lost only 60 percent, yet my statement says I'm way under water!"

My client's mental accounting told him that a gain of 80 percent less a loss of 60 percent should leave him 20 percent ahead. The reality was that his original $1,000,000 investment grew 80 percent to $1,800,000, so his 60 percent loss was on $1,800,000, for a loss of $1,080,000. The end result? A balance of $1,800,000 less $1,080,000 left him with only $720,000. It was a painful way to learn that big losses take much bigger gains to recover.

Consider, for example, a volatile investment of $100,000 that loses 50 percent the first year, leaving you with $50,000. Suppose the next year you make 50 percent, so your average return for the two years is 0 percent. Did you break even? Nope. Your $50,000 grew 50 percent to $75,000, leaving you $25,000 under water. Remember that the next time you want to risk funds in a high flyer.

FRAMING

Kahneman presented much more on the problems investors face because we're human and not necessarily rational. Then he provided us with the hope that we might help our clients (and ourselves) be better investors through the power of *framing*.

Framing has to do with the idea that the way people behave depends on how questions are framed. Suppose I offered you two brands of chocolate bars. One was 90 percent fat free and the other contained 10 percent fat. I'll bet I know which one you'd chose. Have you looked for prunes lately? You may have trouble finding them unless you look for dried plums. The Sunkist marketing department understands framing.

How can you use this technique to be a better investor? Here are a few ideas:

The next time your neighbor gives you a hot tip, instead of focusing on all the good things that might happen, reframe your focus and ask yourself what might go wrong. My partner, Deena, once helped a client make an important decision by pointing out that if she made the significant investment she was considering and it succeeded, she could increase her standard of living by 10 percent. However, if it didn't pan out, she would have to work four years beyond her planned retirement date to make up for the loss. She passed on the opportunity. She may not have made a killing and missed out on taking a world cruise, but she was able to retire just when she wanted to.

Reframe your performance-evaluation horizon. Investing for retirement is investing for the rest of your life, so when evaluating your investment's performance, keep your eye on the long-term, not the daily market gyrations. That means skip the comparisons to last month, last quarter, or year-to-date performance and look at performance over years and market cycles. Also, reframe your benchmark. You might compare your large-cap core manager's performance to the S&P 500 but not to your portfolio. Instead, consider using a real-return benchmark—compare your portfolio return to inflation. After all, that's what your plan should be based on.

Are you holding a position in a stock at a big paper loss, but you're reluctant to sell because then it would be a real loss? If I asked you whether you'd buy that stock today, you'd tell me I'm nuts. You wouldn't touch that dog with a ten-foot pole! Let's reframe your decision. Since the cost of trading today is negligible, you could sell your investment tomorrow and have the cash proceeds in your hand almost immediately. That means by holding onto your stock, you've made the decision to buy it again!

The moral? We're human, not rational, and recognizing reality and learning about some of the problems our biases and heuristics get us into and using framing to help manage these risks will make us far better investors.

CHAPTER 18

FLIGHT TO SAFETY:

———————◆———————

The Portfolio that Makes for an Uncertain Future

CERTAINTY ISN'T SAFE

Harold Evensky (HE): Kirin, good to see you. Where's Autumn?

Kirin (K): She's out shopping. I wanted to see you alone. I'm very upset and concerned about my investments; I don't want her to know and get worried.

HE: Kirin, what's worrying you?

K: Well, as you know, most of my money is in a series of large, one-year CDs that I've been rolling over every year. A few years ago, I was getting almost 9 percent. It's been going down every year, and now I'm facing rolling them into CDs that are paying only 1 percent! Harold, we can't live on 1 percent.

HE: I hear you and, indeed, rates have come down significantly. We might find a bank paying a tad more, but it would be a small increase. Let's talk about repositioning at least some money into a balanced portfolio.

K: A balanced portfolio? That sounds like it has stocks?

HE: Indeed, the idea is to balance your investments between stocks and bonds—probably somewhere in the range of 50 percent bonds and 50 percent stock.

K: Harold, forget it! The market's too risky. No way am I buying stock.

HE: Okay, Kirin, let's talk about designing a laddered bond portfolio.

K: What's that?

HE: Well, we would buy a series of high-quality bonds maturing each year during a period of time. If you invested $100,000, we might buy ten bonds, one maturing in one year, the next in two years, and so on until the last $10,000 was invested in a ten-year bond. That way, if interest rates go up in a year, you'll have the money from the maturing bond to invest at the new higher, ten-year rate, and if rates go down, you'll have most of your money invested in bonds paying a higher return than the current market.

K: Sounds cleaver, but forget it. No way am I tying up my money that long.

HE: Okay, Kirin, I give up. Stop buying your one-year CDs and buy five-year CDs. At least they pay a little bit more.

K: Harold, no way. Long-term to me is a green banana.

HE: *[By now, I was more than a little frustrated.]* Kirin, go ahead make my day—die. *[Normally, I wouldn't be so blunt, but Kirin was not only a client but also a long-time friend and I thought he needed a significant wake-up call, so I went on.]* If you really did die, I would be distraught because you're a good friend, but what keeps me awake at night and should keep *you* awake at night is *not* dying and having no financial assets to support your lifestyle. As my friend Nick Murray would say, your problem is confusing safety and certainty.

CDs are certain in that you can have confidence that you will receive the interest payments promised and your full principal back at maturity. In the real world, the friction of taxes and inflation is likely to result in your certain payments buying less and less. That means your standard of living will gradually be eroded. That is not safe. The moral? Don't confuse certainty and safety. A safe investment portfolio has a high probability of allowing you to maintain your standard of living. For most of us, that means investing in both bonds and stocks.

CHAPTER 19

MARKET TIMING:

A Fool's Game

Markets don't care about what you need.

The Trujillos visited me a few months after the technology market crashed in 2002. They were a lovely couple—both in their mid-seventies—Mr. Trujillo was dapper in his tailored blue blazer, and Mrs. Trujillo was beautifully coiffed and dressed in a lovely St. John suit (my wife's favorite high-end store). They had scheduled the meeting after sustaining significant losses during the tech market crash. After the traditional introductory "how are you" courtesies, Mr. Trujillo came right to the point.

Mr. Trujillo (T): Mr. Evensky, our investments were decimated in the market crash and we're desperate to recover those losses. We've cut our expenses to the bone. The only basic needs remaining are our club and golf dues and our annual cruise. We're hoping that you, as a professional, can help us.

Harold Evensky (HE): Mr. Trujillo, I'm sorry to hear about your losses. Perhaps you can give me some idea of how you believe I may be of help?

Mr. T: Well, we thought that by judicious market timing and sophisticated stock picking we can earn returns well beyond what we could by just tracking the market.

HE: I understand. Tell me how you were investing prior to the market crash.

Mr. T: Given the extraordinary returns in technology and all of the news about the new era of the nineties, we were heavily concentrated in technology funds. We recognized the risk of putting all of our eggs in one basket, so we diversified among several well-respected technology funds. For a year, we were doing extremely well; our returns were more than 80 percent. Unfortunately, no one warned us prior to the market crash, and in less than a year our portfolio was down 70 percent! I still don't understand why we lost so much. It seems that if we made 80 percent and lost 70 percent, we should still be 10 percent ahead.

HE: I understand. Let me do some analyses to see how you're positioned so I can determine what recommendations may be appropriate. Can we get together next week?

Mr. T: That would be fine.

After the Trujillos left, I gathered the information they had provided regarding their current investments and all of their financial goals. Factoring in assumptions for taxes, future market returns, and inflation, I entered all of the information into our planning software, MoneyGuide Pro, and ran several scenarios with varying allocations between bonds and stocks.

It was bad news: no matter how I jiggled the allocations, my conclusion was the Trujillos could reasonably spend only about one-half of what they considered a bare-bones lifestyle. That's not the sort of news a planner looks forward to sharing with a client. Unfortunately, although Mr. Trujillo said they needed a return that would enable them to maintain their lifestyle, the reality is that the markets don't give a damn.

How about Mr. Trujillo's solution of market timing? As I explained to David Samuel in Chapter 14, "Market Timing for Fun and Someone Else's Profit," trying to find the pot of gold at the end of the rainbow is not a viable investment strategy. Unfortunately, their experience with the boom and bust of their portfolio didn't convince them of the market-timing fallacy. Rather than the impossibility of consistently making the right call on market turns, Mr. Trujillo complained that no one warned them prior to the market crash. He ignored the fact that no one warned him because no one *knew* in advance. If you think about it, had the impending crash been obvious to professional investors, they would have moved to cash prior to the crash. Of course, they didn't, and across the board, professionals, including the managers of the Trujillos' diversified funds, were blindsided, as both investors and professionals have been with every market correction and crash.

You may be thinking about people you know who managed to avoid much of the loss during a bear market, and I'm sure that's true. In fact, one of the major arguments for active management is that it may not work all of the time, but it comes to the forefront during bear markets because an active manager can reduce his or her equity exposure, whereas an index fund must stay fully invested. Although that statement is true, the conclusion is not.

In 2013, my graduate assistant (who's now a professor), Shaun Pfeiffer, and I researched this argument. We found two fatal flaws: 1) The majority of active managers did not avoid bear market losses. 2) Even more importantly, those who managed to avoid losses in one bad market generally fail to do so in subsequent bad markets.

As for Mr. Trujillo's confusion about his loss versus his expected 10 percent gain, it's a classic—and dangerous—mental math trap. Big losses have far greater ramifications than most investors understand. Suppose the portfolio was valued at $1,000,000 before the big 80 percent gain. It would have grown to $1,800,000. If it then lost 70 percent, the 70 percent was a loss on the $1,800,000 portfolio, leaving a balance of only $540,000! Even worse, to get back to the $1,000,000, the Trujillos would need an 85 percent return. Not likely.

What did I tell the Trujillos? As tactfully as I could, I walked them through the numbers and tried to explain the reality of their financial position. Unfortunately, I was unsuccessful and they continued to insist that having cut expenses to the bone, they would have to simply find someone who could help. I wished them the best but feared they would simply be digging themselves into a deeper hole with progressively less opportunity to at least mitigate the pain.

The moral? Markets don't have feelings or morals. They do not care what an investor needs and there is no investment or strategy that has consistently provided returns well in excess of those earned in the broad markets. Consequently, if you care about your financial future, don't base the quality of your life on hopes, dreams, and the expectation of being the first person to find that pot of gold or win the lottery. Do your planning based on the reality of the markets.

CHAPTER 20

DANGEROUS MEASURES:

━━━━━━◆━━━━━━

The Fine Art of Calculating Returns

The person responsible for translating the math chapter of my book, *Wealth Management,* into Japanese told me, "You give me much headache." Welcome to the math chapter.

Okay, class, today we're going to be discussing one of the most common activities for financial planners, namely, the calculation of investment returns. Accounting in some measurable way for changes in investment values is fundamental to the work of financial planners. It may come as a surprise to you that such a simple concept is fraught with danger. The danger lies in the potential misuse of valid measurements.

There wouldn't be much room for confusion if there were only one valid measure of investment return. Unfortunately, the mathematics of finance offers many choices. Among the most common are:

- Current return

- Total return (holding period return)

- Real return

- Compounded return

- Time-weighted return

- Dollar-weighted return (internal rate of return (IRR) and modi-fied IRR)

- Arithmetic return

- Risk-adjusted return

- Sharp ratio

Let's consider each and I'll simplify the discussion by assuming that we're referring to the income received for a full year.

CURRENT RETURN

This is perhaps the most popular measure with investors and some mutual fund marketing mavens. It is frequently referred to as the *yield* or *payout*. It's an attractive measure because it provides a simple measure of the annual payout on an investment.

$$\text{Current return} = \frac{\text{Total income received for the year}}{\text{Investment}}$$

Although simple, this measure has a major problem. Consider the number we use for total income. That single number doesn't distinguish the nature of the income. Is it interest income or principal payments, or capital gains, or some combination of those? There's no way of knowing how consistent an income stream will be in the future. I'll promise to pay you a current return of 20 percent per year as long as you don't ask me for any money after five years.

$$\text{Yield} = \frac{\text{Interest income received for the year}}{\text{Investment}}$$

Okay, let's focus on the interest income. Will that resolve the problem? Not necessarily. The bond fund we've invested in may hold many premium bonds. Those are bonds that were issued when interest rates were much higher, so although we receive significant current annual income, some of that is actually a return of principal. When bonds mature they will be paid off at par not at the bonds' current market premium value.

Now we can talk about some measures that may be more useful.

$$\text{Total return} = \frac{\text{Income + realized and unrealized capital gains - any capital loss}}{\text{Investment}}$$

This simple measure eliminates potential misleading factors that affect current return, but it fails to answer a number of important questions. Measuring total return is only a starting point in evaluating investment returns.

REAL RATE OF RETURN = TOTAL RETURN MINUS INFLATION RATE

Another simple but very important calculation determines what investment advisors call "real return"—how much did an investor actually make after inflation. Earning 10 percent if inflation is 3 percent would be nice, but if a few years later inflation is 8 percent and they're still earning 10 percent total return, that wouldn't be so nice. All our clients live in the real world, so all of your planning should be based on an "after inflation" real return.

COMPOUNDED RETURN

Now we're getting to the number most investors are looking for: "What did I earn last year?" The most common measure is called the Internal Rate of Return (IRR). It's also known as the dollar-weighted return. This calculation considers the timing of additional investments your clients made and/or withdrawals they took during the year and the return of the investments in the portfolio.

TIME VERSUS DOLLAR-WEIGHTED RETURN

We're not done yet, one more to go. The power of IRR to include interim additions and withdrawals from the portfolio is also its Achilles' heel. If you're evaluating the performance of a portfolio when you have control of the external cash flows, the IRR provides a valid measure. If you have no control of the external cash flows—when your client adds or withdraws money—you need to consider using two measures. The IRR will provide a valid measure of your client's portfolio performance; however, it will not answer the question of how successful your recommendations were.

To answer that question, you need an alternative investment-return calculation known as the Time-Weighted Return (TWR). Basically, this measure calculates how the investment would have performed if no new additions or withdrawals had been made during the year. After all, if you and your selected money managers have no control of the timing of external cash flows, your performance should not be penalized (or rewarded) for your client's unfortunate (or fortunate) investment timing.

For example, consider the results of two investors, each of whom invested in the same mutual fund. Investor A invested $90 at the beginning of year one and an additional $10 at the beginning of year four. Investor B placed $10 in the portfolio at the beginning of year one and $90 at the beginning of year four. Here are the results of their investments:

Year-End	INVESTOR A Investment	Portfolio Value	INVESTOR B Investment	Portfolio Value
INITIAL	$90		$10	
1		$108	$12	
2		$97		$10
3		$97		$10
4	$10	$139 $90		$121
5		$153		$144
Average annual return		10.6%		8.8%
Internal rate of return		9.4%		16.7%
(or dollar weight)				
Time-weighted return		9.0%		9.0%

So there you have it, two investors, investing in the same portfolio, resulting in six different performance numbers. What do those numbers tell us? The average annual return? Not much. The dollar-weighted return? Investor B was lucky and invested the bulk of his money at opportune times and the advice was credited with a 9 percent annualized return.

CHAPTER 21

MANAGING RISK:

———————◆———————

Smart Ways to Avoid the Bad and Manage the Good

Come and join me again in my Wealth Management class.

Good morning, everyone. I hope you all had a great spring break. Anyone do something especially fun?"

"Professor E, I went home to Istanbul to visit family. It was all too short a trip but it was wonderful seeing everyone, as I'd not been home in a long time." [That was my ace teaching assistant, Cagla.]

"Henry, how about you?"

"Well, I've been working on my dissertation, so I hunkered down to move it along. I still have a lot to do but it feels good having such a good start."

"Excellent. Is everyone ready to get back to the best class in the program? *[Needless to say, the class offers a resounding confirmation.]*

Okay, this afternoon we're going to begin with a discussion about two Nobel laureates, Harry Markowitz and William Sharpe. I know you all have thoroughly read the assigned material including some of their seminal works, so my question is this: how would you describe the significance of their work to a client? Katie, why don't you start with Professor Markowitz?

Katie: Professor Markowitz recognized that in investing we need to consider risk as well as return. That may seem pretty obvious today, but at the time, the sole focus of investors was on which investment would provide the highest return. To the extent risk that was considered at all, investments were simply categorized as conservative or speculative. In fact, for decades, there were lists of legally approved, "safe" investments for fiduciaries such as banks and trusts. For our clients, the significant insight Markowitz introduced was the concept that a well-designed portfolio of individually risky investments could actually result in a safer portfolio. Professor Evensky, may I use the blackboard to demonstrate?

HE: Of course.

Katie: Okay, picture two very volatile investments. Although we expect that over the long-term their returns will be positive, on an annual basis their returns may vary significantly. Basically, this is our expectation of traditional investments such as stocks.

Here's a simple example:

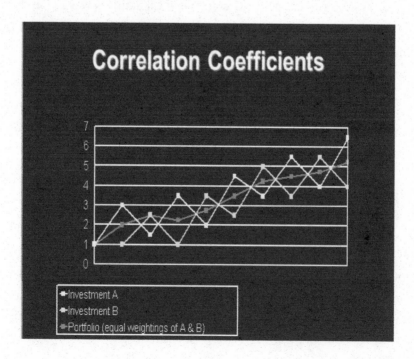

Although stocks A and B are both very volatile, they both trend up. As my graph demonstrates, if we were to invest half of our portfolio in A and half in B, we'd end up with an overall portfolio with almost no volatility. Unfortunately, in the real world, we can't find investments that complement each other so perfectly, but we *can* find investments that don't move in exactly the same pattern, or as a mathematician would say, investments that are poorly correlated. That's the wisdom that Professor Markowitz introduced. So today we don't think in terms of risky investments but rather in terms of complementary investments; that's why professional advisors and wise investors are so focused on portfolio diversification.

HE: Well done, Katie. David, how would you explain Professor Sharpe's contribution to your clients?

David: Well, I'd start with this picture:

INVESTMENT RISK

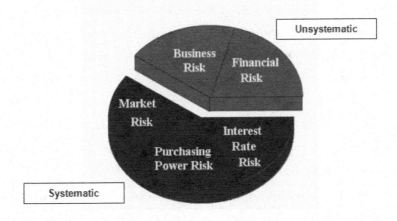

Professor Sharpe demonstrated that there are two fundamental types of risk—unsystematic and systematic. Unsystematic risks are those uniquely associated with individual investments. This kind of risk is considered unrewarded because it's risk that provides no expectation of extra return.

There are many reasons an individual investment might fail. A company may be badly managed and go belly up, or it might be well managed but fall prey to unfortunate market conditions, such as an energy company facing a collapse in oil prices. From the investor's standpoint, it doesn't matter whether the business failure is due to poor management or market forces. If the business fails, the investor is the loser.

At least theoretically, an investor may eliminate this unsystematic risk by diversifying. For example, a real estate investor owning and renting out a single-family home that ends up unoccupied would face a total loss of income, but if he or she owned ten homes, a single vacancy would mean only a 10 percent loss. Here's what unsystematic risk looks like in the stock market:

April 20, 2010 – BP Deepwater Horizon Oil Spill

Stock Price April 20, 2010 ……..………………. $50.20

Stock Price Three months later ………………... $28.74

I can buy a portfolio of five hundred of the bluest blue chips—all the stocks in the S&P 500—but if the market drops 20 percent, that means my diversified blue chip portfolio took a major beating. In my pie graph, that risk is the first wedge of systematic risk—market risk. Many investors say, "I know that and that's why I buy only high-quality municipal bonds." Well, as we know, bonds are subject to something called interest rate risk. That means if I buy a bond and a few years later interest rates go up, the value of my bond goes down.

Some astute investors respond by saying, "I know that. That's why I buy only one-year CDs and roll them over. That way, when rates go up, I get the new, higher return." That also sounds as if it makes sense, but rates can go down and the investor's income can drop precipitously. That risk is called reinvestment risk. (See Chapter 18, "Flight to Safety.") So, although many investors think of bonds as a simple, safe alternative to stocks, the reality is that they come with their own unique kinds of risks.

Finally, there is the last wedge—purchasing power erosion. We all know that throughout time the costs of things we buy and the services we need go up due to inflation. That's the other real risk of depending on bond income as the sole source of cash flow. Many investors get in trouble by confusing certainty with safety. Bond returns may be certain, but when you factor in inflation as a primary source of income, they're certainly not safe.

HE: David, well done. I believe your future clients will be well served by your educating them about the wisdom of the laureates.

CHAPTER 22

THE EFFICIENT FRONTIER:

How Much Risk Can You Stomach?

Anchoring on the efficient frontier may sound like something out of Star Trek, but it's not. It's better.

Harold Evensky (HE): Mr. and Mrs. Curtis, good morning. I'm Harold Evensky and this is my partner, Matt McGrath. Welcome to Evensky & Katz. I always like to start by asking, "What brings y'all here?"

Mr. Curtis (Mr. C): Well, Harold, Vickie and I are thinking about retiring in just a few years. We've saved quite a bit and think we'll be in good shape, but we had some friends who retired a few years ago, who thought they were in good shape only to discover that things didn't work out quite as well as they expected and they've had to do some major cutting back in their lifestyle. We don't want that to happen to us. The Hamptons said you helped them do some planning for their retirement so we thought we'd like to work with you to do the same.

HE: Wonderful. Let's have some fun envisioning your future. And that's the key—it's *your* future. Our job is to empower you to plan that future. Suppose we start off with an introduction: "Modern Portfolio Theory and You." Matt, may I have a blank sheet of paper from your pad? Thanks.

Here's a simple picture of the investment world. On one axis, we'll plot *risk* and on the other, *return*.

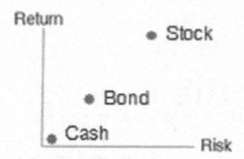

As you'd expect, *cash* would not be very risky, but it would not provide much in the way of return, whereas *stock* might provide a high return but at some risk. *Bonds* are somewhere in between.

With just these three choices, we could still design thousands of portfolios. For example, 99 percent bonds and 1 percent stock or 99 percent stock and 1 percent bonds. If I put dots on my graph for the risk and return combinations of all of these combinations, I'd fill up the picture with dots. Then, if I drew a line enclosing all of those dots, I would end up with a curved line that's called the *efficient frontier*.

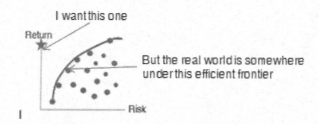

That means, at least theoretically, there is no *best* portfolio but rather an infinite number of best portfolios, depending on the risk one is willing to take. We know that everyone would like to have a portfolio with no risk and lots of return. Unfortunately, the real world of potential portfolios lies on or below the efficient frontier. So what does that mean for you?

Well, it means we have to do some planning, and then you'll have a decision to make. First, as I said starting off, we need to make a best guess as to what return your portfolio would need to earn over time to provide you the money you need to accomplish all of your retirement goals. Then we need to make a best guess as to your risk tolerance. If we just focused on your return needs, we might conclude it was possible to achieve your financial goals with a portfolio allocated 90 percent to stock. But that might not work out very well if we faced a major bear market in a few years. After you saw your nest egg lose 40 percent, you'd call us and say, "Harold, we can't stand it. Please sell our stock and put our money in cash!"

That's why we define *risk tolerance* as the point of pain and misery you can survive—with us holding onto your belt and suspenders—just before you make that call to tell us to sell out.

With those two anchors, we can now revisit our graph. Suppose the results look like this.

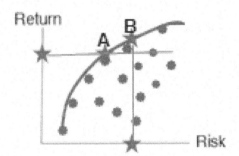

We have two portfolios for you. Portfolio A is one that provides the return you need to achieve your goals, and B is one in keeping with your risk tolerance. Which one is right? In fact, both are, but our recommendation is to plan on Portfolio A. Why? Even though we believe you can live with more risk and would end up with more money, determining risk tolerance well in advance of a terrible market is more art than science. The consequence if we're wrong and you bail out of the market that would be catastrophic. So why take that extra risk if you don't need it to achieve your goals?

How about if we found a different outcome? Suppose we concluded that you needed Portfolio A to provide your needed return but had a risk tolerance associated with Portfolio B in this picture.

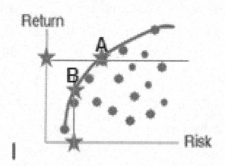

That's not very good, because now you have to decide between eating less or sleeping less. In this case, our recommendation would be to readjust your goals to meet the return expectations of Portfolio B. Why? Again, when markets seem okay, it's all too easy to say, "I'll take a bit more risk." But later, when it seems the world is coming to an end, you're not likely to remember your willingness to hang in there.

CHAPTER 23

LAGNIAPPE:

———————◆———————

Some Final Takeaways

I couldn't resist using one of my favorite words—*lagniappe*. It means a little something extra, given at no cost, somewhat like the thirteenth doughnut in a baker's dozen. Because there are so many topics and issues I could not cover in the previous chapters, here's my lagniappe.

Small and Ugly May Be Beautiful. If you need more returns. One possible strategy, supported by decades of research, is to overweight a few market factors in your portfolio. Based on the original research of two well-known academics, Gene Fama and Ken French, you allocate some of your stock holdings to small companies and value stock. Over the long-term, you're likely to be rewarded with a few extra percentage points of returns.

Maximize Quality of Life, Not Returns. It's confusing, but after having designed many hundreds of retirement plans, it's obvious that if you're near or in retirement and depending on your portfolio to provide cash flow for your lifestyle, a higher allocation to bonds is likely to increase your likelihood of success at the cost of reducing the likelihood of making more money.

Hot Stocks Pay. If you're an active trader in hot stocks, the activity will pay your broker but not you. Remember two old jokes: 1) Broker to a new client pointing out the window of his beautiful office overlooking the bay.

"See that yacht; that's my partner's. The one next to it is Mark's—he's the broker next door—and the one next to that is mine." The wise prospect asks, "Where are the clients' yachts?" 2) How do I make a $1,000,000 in the market? Start with $2,000,000.

Safety versus Certainty. My friend Nick Murray shakes his head when he hears people talking about safe investments. He says (and he's right): investors confuse *safety* with *certainty.* Putting your nest egg into insured CDs may offer the certainty that when they mature, you get your principal back with the promised interest; however, assuming you're like most of us and find your expenses going up with inflation, over time your safe investment is likely to buy you less and less of the goods and services you need. This is called purchasing power erosion and it's one of the biggest risks retirees face. The solution is to plan on a safe portfolio—one with bonds and stocks—and avoid the certainty of losing purchasing power with a safe investment.

It Doesn't Cost You Anything Don't You Believe It. Unless you're the kind of person who believes in fairy tales. No professional can afford to work for free. Good investment advice is valuable, and people providing advice deserve and expect to be compensated. So it really angers me when an investor says they were told a service shouldn't cost them anything.

Two prime examples are bonds and variable annuities. When purchasing a bond, it's true that you're not charged a commission. That doesn't mean you're not paying compensation. Bonds are sold based on something called a spread. You might be offered a $10,000 bond at 102.5. That means your cost would be $10,250. The broker may have been told by his bond department: "This bond is available at 100.5. How much do you want to add?" To which the broker responds, "Two." And the trader says, "Fine. Done at 102.5." The result: you're purchasing a bond with a 2 percent markup. The markup is the fee to the broker and brokerage firm. Again, there's nothing wrong with paying a markup, but make sure you're told how much it is. The good news is that you can check by going to http://

finramarkets.morningstar.com/MarketData/Default.jsp , a website that provides the details of most bond trades.

A Variable Annuity (VA) is another investment product that, unfortunately, a small minority of unscrupulous brokers use to take advantage of clients. The line is: "Don't worry. It doesn't cost you anything. The insurance company pays me." Although factually true, it's massively misleading because it ignores the reality of where the insurance company gets the money to pay the broker. The money comes from you, the annuity purchaser. The practice is particularly egregious because VAs typically pay relatively high commissions to brokers and they have no break points, unlike mutual funds. On mutual funds the commission drops as the purchase size gets larger. The broker gets the same percentage on a VA no matter how big the purchase.

Duration, Shmuration. Who Cares? You should. You probably know, or at least have heard (especially if you read Chapter 7, "Getting Your Money Back"), that bonds are subject to interest rate risk. That's the risk of being stuck with a poor investment if after having purchased a bond, interest rates rise.

Consider John, new owner of a $10,000 ten-year bond purchased when it was paying 4 percent. Five years later, interest rates are up and a new five-year bond of the same quality now pays 7 percent. If John wishes to sell his bond, he would be offering his now five-year bond paying 4 percent. There is no way someone will pay him $10,000 for a bond paying 4 percent when the buyer can purchase a similar quality bond paying 7 percent. So if the owner, John, wants to sell, he'd have to sell at a discount.

That discount is *interest rate risk*. Most investors equate this risk with maturity—they assume a ten-year bond has significantly greater risk than a five-year bond. Sounds reasonable but it's not necessarily true. The problem is that focusing only on maturity leaves out an important factor—the coupon, which is how much the bond issuer pays annually. The higher the coupon, the sooner the investor has some funds back to reinvest at the new, higher rate so a high-coupon bond might have less interest rate risk than a shorter-maturity, low-coupon bond. For an approximate guide to the level of interest rate risk a bond has, ask about the bond's duration. That number will provide a very rough guide to the potential loss in value if rates rise. The measure is 1 percent for every year of duration. So a bond with a five-year duration might be expected to lose 5 percent if rates go up 1 percent or 10 percent if rates rise 2 percent. Not a perfect measure but far better than maturity.

I'll Keep an Eye on It. When I caution clients about the risk of a heavy concentration in a single investment, they often respond, "Harold, I understand, but I keep a careful eye on it." That sounds wise. Unfortunately, as Professor Sharpe taught us about the unrewarded diversifiable risk, that's false confidence. It's a risk that can blindside you.

Think about the fact that many years ago a crazy person who put poison in some Tylenol bottles threatened the business of Johnson & Johnson or consider the Gulf oil disaster that almost buried BP. Years ago, I used to use as the example of a company building a major manufacturing facility over what turned out to be a toxic waste dump. Well, one day, using that story to persuade my clients to reduce their exposure to the stock they held in the company where they had both spent their careers.

Their mouths dropped open and they said, "Good Lord! You're right! We'll sell out." It turned out that just a few years earlier their company had, in fact, developed a major research facility over what later turned out to be a toxic dump and it almost bankrupted the firm.

It doesn't matter how blue the blue chip is, the risk is there. Many years ago I warned a trustee that a portfolio allocation to AT&T stock representing about half the portfolio value was a significant risk. Unfortunately, I wasn't very persuasive and the trustee scoffed at my warning—after all, it was AT&T. About a year later the value dropped over 50 percent. The drop had nothing to do with my having a crystal ball; it might just as well have doubled in price. The point is that the risk is real.

Counting on Gurus to Predict the Future May Be Hazardous to Your Wealth. No question about it: when doing investment planning, you need to have some opinion about future market returns. In my office, I have all of the important elements, including extensive databases, sophisticated analytical software, an expensive crystal ball, and a Ouija board. The future is mighty cloudy and surprises even the best of us.

The moral? It's not Buy and hold, it's Buy and Manage. Make your best estimates about the future and be prepared to change. Just don't put too much faith in any guru's ability to tell you where the market's going, no matter how confident he or she may be.

THAT'S ALL FOLKS

I hope you've enjoyed sharing my stories and that at least a few resonate with you. I know that integrating the knowledge of these vignettes in your personal planning will make you a better investor. I wish you a healthy, happy, and financially secure future.

Harold